THE ULTIMATE NUMEROLOGY BOOK

THE COMPLETE GUIDE TO THE SPIRITUAL MEANING OF NUMBERS INCLUDING HOW YOUR BIRTHDAY AND NAME AFFECT YOUR LIFE PATH

DELPHINA WOODS

HENTOPAN
PUBLISHING

CONTENTS

A Special Offer
From Hentopan Publishing

Get this additional book from Delphina Woods just for joining the Hentopan Launch Squad.

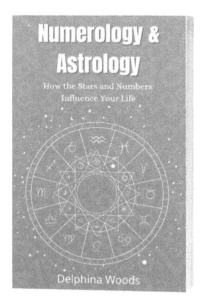

Get your free electronic copy by scanning the QR code below with your phone.

RESOURCES

Pythagorean Alphanumeric Cipher

1	2	3	4	5	6	7	8	9
A	B	C	D	E	F	G	H	I
J	K	L	M	N	O	P	Q	R
S	T	U	V	W	X	Y	Z	

Significance of Numbers

1	2	3	4
The Primal Force	**The Divine Feminine**	**The Enthusiast**	**The Salt of the Earth**
Beginnings	Balance	Creativity	Foundations
Pioneering	Partnership	Jo	Pragmatism
Willpower	Intuition	Communication	Problem Solving
Independence	Diplomacy	Self-expression	Hard Work

5	6	7	8
The Dynamo	**The Caretaker**	**The Seeker**	**The Success Story**
Freedom	Harmony	Spirituality	Wealth
Adventure	Service	Intellect	Ambition
Innovation	Domesticity	Personal growth	Manifestation
Risk	Healing	Solitude	Leadership

9	11	22	33
The Humanitarian	**The Master Dreamer**	**The Master Builder**	**The Master Teacher**
Wisdom	Intuition	Power	Compassion
Awakening	Illumination	Materialization	Understanding
Completion	Potential	Foundations	Responsibility
Self-sacrifice	Anxiety	Pressure	Suffering

INTRODUCTION

Numbers are everywhere – and not only the numbers we can see, like those on our clocks, calculators, and keyboards, but *hidden* numbers. Everything that exists physically and chemically is composed of numbers; they are the most basic building blocks of the universe. Behind even the atom and its subatomic particles, there are numbers that, through their unique energy frequencies, inform every aspect of existence – from the planets and the stars all the way down to your birth.

Numerology allows us to harness the power of these universal building blocks. Through understanding the meanings of the numbers that lie hidden in your name, birthday, and other dates, numerology can help you paint a picture of what exactly makes you, *you* – as well as what your future holds.

I first began experimenting with numerology some years ago, when I was at a particularly challenging point in my life. I had just experienced a drastic change in living situation, was laid off from my career, *and* my relationship fell apart – all at once. I was feeling more than a little bit lost in life, and I was so desperate for guidance, I was willing to try anything – but what I found in my numerological chart astounded me.

Numerology didn't just offer me guidance on how to overcome the challenges I was facing: my chart laid out *everything about me.* My pinnacles and challenges reflected what I had just been through, and I was able to conceptualize this difficult time in my life as the turning point from one cycle to the next.

I realized that my life had fallen apart because I was being called to do something greater – this wasn't the end for me, but the beginning. Along with honest intro-spection, my numerological chart empowered me to turn my weaknesses into strengths, align my actions with my higher purpose, and prepare for the next chal-lenges on my horizon.

I'm writing this book today because I am called to help you find the same understanding and sense of empow-erment. In the following chapters, I'll walk you step-by-step through calculating all the principal numbers in your own numerological chart and I'll clearly explain with words what each one means for you and your life. No confusing colors or occult symbols, no blathering esoteric jargon – just simple, powerful, elegant truths that will undoubtedly speak to you as they did to me.

Whatever you may be facing in life, I know in my soul that numerology can help you overcome it. The numbers in your chart reflect the energies *already inherent in you*. You have everything you need at your fingertips.

Let me teach you to harness it!

1

NUMEROLOGY 101

Since you've picked up this book, I suspect you are eager to unlock the mysteries of numerology and to learn all that this ancient art can teach you about yourself and your destiny – and we'll get there, I promise! First, though, let's begin with the basics.

In this chapter, we'll cover the *what* and *why* of numerology, only briefly touching on the *how*. This will lay a solid foundational understanding of numerology on which you'll build a repertoire of calculations as you progress through the book.

What is Numerology?

Numerology is the study of the spiritual or supernatural significance of numbers. You can think of numerology as "divination by numbers," much the same as astrology is divination by celestial bodies. A numerologist studies the influence that numbers have on our lives, and, as in astrology, the wisdom gleaned from this study may guide decision-making and equip the practitioner with a better understanding of their core being, enabling them to better navigate their life path and their relationships – in other words, to meet their fullest potential.

The central tenets of numerology are that numbers have innate vibrational energy and that all things can be represented in numerical form. In fact, the Greek philosopher Pythagoras, for whom the famous Pythagorean theorem is named, proclaimed that all of existence can be reduced or broken down into single digits – that the numbers 1 through 9 are the metaphysical building blocks of the universe.

If numbers have an innate spiritual meaning and represent all of existence, it follows that, by understanding the specific meanings and spiritual energies of these digits and making the appropriate calculations, numerologists can harness the power of numbers to make predictions and gain insight. In this way, numerology can help us better ourselves and the world around us.

Numerology is distinct from the discipline of mathematics – although, in ancient times, the two studies were much more closely related than they are today – and you don't need to know calculus to benefit from this ancient practice of divination. In fact, as you will learn as you calculate your own numerological chart with the help of this book, the calculations involved in the practice of numerology are exceedingly simple.

Numerological Calculations

In numerology, calculations are done by way of natural addition; that is, adding the component digits of a number from left to right to produce a single-digit sum. If your sum is greater than 9, you'll add the digits again – as many times as needed until you reach a single digit. For example, to calculate the single-digit natural sum of 1997:

$$1997 = 1 + 9 + 9 + 7 = 26 = 2 + 6 = 8$$

And that's it. Of course, there *are* a few exceptions – numbers that are significant in their double-digit form and should not be broken down when they are found in a numerological chart – but these are rare. We'll cover these master numbers in detail later.

When it comes to words rather than numbers, such as in an individual's birth name, numerologists use an alphanumeric cipher, or key, to translate each letter of the alphabet into its single-digit correspondent. Several such keys are available, but the most commonly used today is based on the work of Pythagoras (more on him to come soon).

The Pythagorean numerological alphabet looks like this:

1	2	3	4	5	6	7	8	9
A	B	C	D	E	F	G	H	I
J	K	L	M	N	O	P	Q	R
S	T	U	V	W	X	Y	Z	

So, for example, my first name, Delphina, is summed as follows:

$$D\ E\ L\ P\ H\ I\ N\ A = 4 + 5 + 3 + 7 + 8 + 9 + 5 + 1 = 42 = 4 + 2 = 6$$

These two steps – natural addition and, if necessary, translating letters into numbers – comprise all the numerological calculations in this book. What changes in each calculation is not the process but the *significance* of the calculated digit and its *specific effects* on you and aspects of your life. You can see that, at its core, the practice of numerology is quite simple – no theoretical math degree required!

A series of such calculations go into each individual's numerological chart. A full chart contains a lot of numbers, but perhaps the most important of these are what numerologists call your core numbers. These five numbers are calculated from your name and birthdate, and they hold great influence over all aspects of your life and self. The five core numbers include your birthday number, life path number, expression number, personality number, and soul urge number. We'll cover all these in detail in the next two chapters.

NUMEROLOGY THROUGH HISTORY

Numerology has been around as long as human beings have recognized and used numbers. Numerological practices (if we are to take a broad definition of the term) are culturally and religiously significant in many parts of the world. The sacred meanings of numbers seem to be an intrinsic concept in the human experience, as numerological systems have been developed independently of one another in civilizations around the globe.

The ancient Egyptians, Mayans, and Celts all revered numbers as sacred in one way or another. Kabbalah numerology grew from ancient Hebrew mysticism; the Arabs practiced Abjad, a numerological system that formed the basis of much of Middle Eastern science; The I Ching, a sacred Chinese text, assigns spiritual values to numbers; and even the Bible has the Book of Numbers.

Modern western numerology blends aspects of several ancient systems but is largely based on the work of Greek philosopher Pythagoras, who himself based his teachings on what is called Chaldean numerology – so it is with the ancient Babylonians that we will begin our history of numerology.

Numerology in the Cradle of Civilization

Ancient Mesopotamia was the birthplace of a wealth of human knowledge, including mathematics, astronomy, astrology, and numerology. As far back as 3200 BC, the Sumerians developed the numerical system on which later Mesopotamian mathematics and numerology were based.

The name Chaldean numerology comes from the Chaldean people, who believed their ancestry was not altogether human, but divine. The Chaldean dynasty ruled the ancient city of Babylon, which became the Neo-Babylonian Empire, historically known as the Chaldean Empire, before it fell to Persia. Chaldean numerology actually predates the Chaldean rule of Mesopotamia.

To the ancient Mesopotamians, the numbers 1 through 8 hold sacred meaning, and 9 is the most sacred of all. Double-digit numbers were believed to represent a person's inner life, while single-digit numbers were said to represent a person's outward persona.

Ancient Mesopotamian numerologists believed that a person's name and birthday should always be in harmony – and since birth dates are immutable, the Mesopotamian people believed strongly in choosing the perfect name for a person at birth.

When Alexander the Great conquered Mesopotamia in 330 BC, he brought back to Egypt great knowledge from the birthplace of civilization. While studying in Egypt, the Greek thinker Pythagoras learned of Chaldean numerology. Pythagoras studied the system of Mesopotamian numbers for many years, eventually adapting it into his own system and imparting considerable Greek influence.

Pythagorean Numerology

Pythagoras was a venerated Greek mathematician and philosopher in the 6th century BCE, whose name is still heard in classrooms across the world today. He is best known for his Pythagorean theorem, a geometric equation that calculates the hypotenuse of a right triangle, for which he has been dubbed the father of geometry – but what you may *not* have learned in grade school math class is that Pythagoras was *also* the father of modern numerology.

Pythagoras studied Chaldean numerology and mathematics for over twenty years in Egypt, and he is said to have actually been captured and taken to Babylon. While a captive in Mesopotamia, Pythagoras partnered with a Zoroastrian priest to study the harmonies of the universe. There, Pythagoras discovered the relationship between music and numbers.

Pythagoras's breakthrough led him to understand that the universe is built on the power of numbers. He believed that all phenomena can be reduced to the numbers 1 through 9 and that these numbers correspond to universal vibrations, containing the essence of all that exists in both the world of man and the world of the spirit – and modern science now confirms that Pythagoras and other ancient mystics were correct in their belief that everything in the universe vibrates.

Pythagoras created his numerological system by pairing each letter of the Greek alphabet with a corresponding number 1 through 9. He and his students used this system to calculate the divinatory meaning of written words. Sadly, Pythagoras's teachings were not written down; we know what we do of his work only from the writings of his students.

Numerology in the Dark Ages

As the Christian Church rose to power, numerology began to fall out of favor, along with astrology and other newly-labeled occult practices. After the First Council of Nicea in 325 AD, the Christian church banned numerology in the Roman Empire, making it a civil violation to practice divination by numbers as Pythagoras and his students taught. The dark ages followed, during which numerology and other occult arts were repressed and practiced only in secret in the western world.

Christianity, however, is no stranger to the sacred meanings of numbers. Ancient Hebrew Kabbalah numerology influenced Christianity before its founding, and while the founders of the early Christian church condemned "mystical" numerology, they *themselves* practiced a form of numerology, ascribing "holy" rather than "occult" meanings to numbers and using these meanings in their interpretations of Christian texts.

For example, the numbers 3 and 7 are quite significant in the Christian mythos, harkening back to the holy trinity and God's 7 days of creation – and of course, the infamous 666 is called "the mark of the beast."

So, numerology didn't cease to be practiced during the dark ages – it simply underwent a transformation. In the Middle Ages and the Renaissance, neoclassical thinkers linked Greek ideas with the predominating Christian meanings ascribed to numbers, drawing strongly on Biblical associations.

Modern Numerological Resurgence

By Victorian times, the public perception of fortune-telling in Europe had evolved from heretical, pagan practice to a harmless parlor game. Numerology, as we know it today, wasn't popularized until the late 19th and early 20th centuries – in fact, the word "numerology" itself wasn't coined until 1907.

Irish occultist William John Warner, known by his pseudonym Cheiro, was partly responsible for the revival of numerology in the western world. Cheiro learned Chaldean numerology, as well as palmistry and astrology, in India and brought his practices back to London in the nineteenth century. Cheiro served the rich and famous as a fortune teller, reading palms of such celebrities as the Prince of Wales and Mark Twain.

It is Mrs. L. Dow Balliett, however, who brought Pythagoras's theories together with Christian influences at the start of the 20th century to found the western numerological system we know today.

Balliett's student, Juno Jordan, continued her work, going on to publish *The Romance in Your Name* in 1965. This book first laid out many of the numerological calculations still used today. The new age movement in the 1970s helped propel the popularity of Balliett and Jordan's numerology. Since then, many more scholars have written on the subject, taking inspiration from a variety of sources. Still, they owe it all to Jordan's book.

UNIVERSAL VIBRATIONS: THE SIGNIFICANCE OF NUMBERS

You have learned that the nine single-digit numbers are the foundational building blocks of numerological study – and as Pythagoras first taught us, of all matter and existence. Each of the single-digit numbers represents a collection of traits, spiritual symbols, and divine meaning derived from Pythagoras's study of universal vibrations. For purposes of this book, I will discuss each of these numbers as if it has its own unique personality, much like the signs of the Zodiac, but you should know that we're speaking about the personality of the individual who corresponds to the number.

By studying the spiritual significance of these single-digit numbers, we aim to harken and interpret the profound messages they send us – either in their places in our numerological charts or when they show up meaningfully throughout our lives.

Here, we'll discover the meanings of each number. You can refer back to this section of the book in the future, or flip to the Resources at the beginning of the book for a short and sweet summary.

0: The Cipher

The 0 is not really considered a number in numerology – for one thing, it wasn't *around as a concept* in mathematics during Pythagoras's time. It is like the primordial waters from which all other numbers spring. Spiritually, the 0 is not just *nothing* – it is the infinite, all-encompassing nothingness just before the Big Bang.

The 0 won't show up often in your numerological chart. On the rare occasion it does (principally within the challenge numbers – we'll cover them in Chapter Six), it represents pure potential. The 0 is all or nothing; it is up to you to decide your fate.

1: The Primal Force

Beginnings, pioneering, willpower, independence.

Spiritually, 1 is the number of divine creation and the primal force from which life springs. It symbolizes the origin of the universe, the birth of all that is. As such, 1 is the root of all opportunities in *our* lives, corresponding with motivation and momentum. It empowers us to take control of our lives and chart our own futures.

A true pioneer and a natural leader, the number 1 is known for breaking new ground, paving the way for others to follow. The 1 has a positive outlook, seeing the world as rife with possibilities. Where others see a roadblock, the 1 sees a challenge to be overcome; this is a highly desirable quality that can lead the 1 to great success.

The number 1 is highly self-sufficient; it needs nothing but its own strengths to thrive. Not one to waste time negotiating or opining about abstract ideas, the 1 prefers to go it alone and get it done. As such, this number can come across as abrasive or aggressive.

The 1 is fearless to the point of feeling invincible, but invincible it is not – this tunnel vision of unwavering determination can easily lead to a disastrous end as the 1 ignores the warning signs, forging full speed ahead.

The dark side of the 1's incredible self-drive is self-doubt, hiding within a primal fear of failure. The 1 is at its best when it uses failures as motivation to improve.

2: The Divine Feminine

Balance, partnership, intuition, diplomacy.

The number 2 represents partnership and is a power-fully feminine force. The 2 heralds balance, harmony, and cooperation – but like the divine feminine, it holds great power and is not to be underestimated as weak or frail.

The 2 is like the concept of "the woman behind the powerful man," working unseen and often unthanked to create impressive results through diplomacy. The 2 uses its considerable influence to accomplish its goals rather than brute force.

A born mediator and peacemaker, the highly coopera-tive 2 can see all sides of an issue and empathetically guide others on the "middle path" back to harmony. The 2 sees the strength in diversity and encourages even contrasting energies to join together to create balance.

The 2 picks up on others' energies on a deep, subcon-scious level and uses this empathic understanding to solve problems. All that intuition means that 2s are very sensitive – the tiniest slight can cut 2 to the core.

One pitfall of staying on the middle road is that the 2 can suffer from "analysis paralysis," unable to make a decision that may rock the boat. More passive than assertive, the 2 is prone to staying in an unpleasant situation for too long and putting others' needs above their own in an effort to keep the peace.

3: The Enthusiast

Creativity, joy, communication, self-expression.

The number 3 is like a child at heart; in fact, you can think of this number as the beautiful product of a union between the capable 1 and the diplomatic 2. Its energy is positively youthful, possessing a remarkable zest for life. The 3 embodies innocence and loves to have fun and express joy. What's not to love? The 3 is the apple of everyone's eye.

The 3 dances from one experience to the next, soaking up every bit of possible enjoyment and collecting all types of new friends along the way. Communication and personal connection are deeply prized by the 3, which uses its unbridled charm and charisma to grow a wide circle of friends, lovers, and other kindred spirits.

Bursting with dreams, musings, and ideas, the 3 is eager to share its unique gifts with the world. But the 3 may suffer from shiny object syndrome, finding itself excited by one too many ideas in quick succession, unable to focus on bringing one to completion. The 3's enthusiasm for living life can lead to important work remaining unfinished.

With unparalleled creative energy, the 3 is a natural artist. Music, visual art, poetry – any form of self-expression lies in the 3's domain. Through art, the 3 can communicate its abstract ideas and feelings in situations where words simply will not suffice.

The 3 lives life broadly rather than deeply, preferring superficial relationships to avoid opening itself up to potential negativity. A childlike pursuit of instant gratification is the dark side of the 3's innocence.

4: The Salt of the Earth

Foundations, pragmatism, problem-solving, hard work.

The number 4 possesses a wise, rational, practical energy that imparts a sense of stability and safety to those in its care. It's a no-nonsense number, firmly grounded in reality with a straightforward approach to life. It prefers to stick with tried and tested methods than experiment with new ideas and new ways of doing things – but the 4's ability to accomplish what it sets its mind to is unparalleled in numerology.

For the 4, pragmatism is the root of productivity. Its rational mind helps it make wise choices, develop efficient plans, and make big things happen through good old-fashioned hard work. If you're looking for dependability, the 4 is where it's at. This hardworking, diligent number never wavers from a commitment.

Sure in its convictions, the 4 sticks to its firm sense of right and wrong, and as such, it tends to see the world in black and white, without shades of gray. Once it has made a decision, the 4 adopts its opinion as fact, and is prone to sharing its perspective as gospel without a care for the opinions of others.

The 4 understands the value of stability and endeavors to build a stable foundation in its life. In pursuit of this, the 4 will put significant effort into building secure relationships. The 4 knows one must give the time and effort necessary for results to be seen, so it gladly commits to acts of service to keep things running smoothly.

Because it's inflexible and chooses work over play, the 4 can be a little... well, boring. While the 4 may be perfectly content in its organized life, this may not be so interesting to others.

5: The Dynamo

Freedom, adventure, innovation, risk.

The 5 craves freedom and adventure; it simply *needs* many exciting experiences to find fulfillment. For the 5, life is all about getting out there and finding new experiences, and this number is never afraid to see where the wind will carry it. This is a very admirable quality, as most have intense difficulty navigating change, but the 5 is a master of adaptation – it truly flourishes in environments of change while others flounder.

Highly curious, the 5 cannot be said to suffer from tunnel vision; instead, it searches in every direction for new and interesting things. This leads the 5 to make great discoveries. By learning through experimentation and always remaining curious, the 5 is highly innovative and full of brilliant new ideas.

As a natural-born explorer, the 5 knows that the best way to interact with the world is through the people who inhabit it. This number thrives in social settings of all types. From large groups to intense one-on-ones, the 5 will take every opportunity to engage with someone new to them.

"New" is the key word, however – the 5 suffers from a serious lack of commitment. Its need for freedom leads it to loathe being "tied down," which makes the formation of long-term relationships very difficult. That incredible curiosity translates to "shiny object syndrome," and before a relationship becomes boring, the 5 is already onto someone new. Because it is so easily distracted, the 5 can be seen as unreliable, struggling to carry something through to the end even when others are depending on it.

Going with the flow of life has its downsides, too. The 5 can lack direction or conviction and is prone to taking risks, which come with consequences as well as rewards.

6: The Caretaker

Harmony, service, domesticity, healing.

The 6 embodies the heart; a highly nurturing number, it is all about unconditional love. This number has powerful compassion and empathy. Shining its warmth generously as a beacon of hope for others, the 6 supports, heals, and offers service to those close to it. What a wonderful vibration to have in one's life!

Its devoted nature and natural empathy make the 6 an excellent partner in any kind of relationship. It excels at making others feel comfortable enough to let their guards down and be vulnerable, in turn allowing the 6 to help where it is most needed. If you need a shoulder to lean on, the 6 is a great listener who offers heartfelt advice.

The 6 has a romantic soul and is very affectionate, fluent in all love languages. Combine this with their drive to protect those they love and you have the perfect domestic partner. The 6 can be fiercely protective – while it may seem passive and peace-loving on the surface, if you mess with the 6's family, you're in for it.

Its high ideals for interpersonal harmony are admirable, but the 6 is likely to forget that the real world doesn't always work this way. More assertive energies can easily overpower the passivity of the 6, who would rather please others and keep the peace than speak up and cause a scene.

Likewise, the virtue of compassion makes the 6 prone to self-sacrifice – often giving of itself to those who are undeserving or even abusive. The 6 would do well to prioritize self-care over the needs of others, as one cannot take care of loved ones if they aren't in good physical and spiritual health themselves.

7: The Seeker

Spirituality, intellect, personal growth, solitude.

The 7 is very wise; it knows that not only are mental prowess and intellect necessary for the betterment of the self, but so is *spiritual knowledge*. The 7 seeks knowledge in all its forms. Not satisfied with surface-level frivolities, the 7 goes deep for the buried treasure that is understanding and doesn't stop until it's struck gold.

As such, asking questions is the hallmark of the 7, whose curiosity is insatiable.

The 7 takes an intellectual approach to life, but this number is more intuitive than you might expect. The 7 seeks knowledge, yes, but it does so both outwardly and inwardly. Adept at using both the conscious and subconscious minds to make decisions, the 7 reveals hidden truths by shining its intuitive light in the darkest realms. It follows that the 7 is supremely spiritual, but it has an intimate, personal connection to its faith rather than engaging in organized religion.

Despite its thirst for knowledge, the 7 isn't just a sponge that soaks up data. Its true power lies in its analytical ability; the 7 sorts through and makes meaning of what it finds, separating insights from the detritus, fact from fiction.

The downside to the 7's ever-seeking nature is that it can come across as suspicious to others – all that looking beneath the surface and digging for answers where there may not be any can ruffle some serious feathers. Additionally, others may see the 7 as a secretive soul who doesn't "open up." Not many know the true depth of the 7, not because it's hiding dark secrets but because it simply doesn't prioritize interpersonal relationships.

With its rich inner life, the biggest danger the 7 faces is reclusivity. Because they value study and the acquisition of wisdom over social affairs, they tend to look inward and stay inward. The 7 would do well to let go of the hunt for ultimate truths every once in a while and instead find the value in nurturing its relationships.

8: The Success Story

Wealth, ambition, manifestation, leadership.

Ding ding ding! Lucky number 8 is the winner. The greatest achiever of numerology, the 8 measures its life by its accomplishments, which are many! This number symbolizes tremendous prosperity and success in business. The association with material wealth and success is so strong that numerologists have been known to change their names to create more 8s in their charts, and in Chinese culture, 8s are worked intentionally into important dates and addresses.

To say the 8 is ambitious would be an understatement. Driven by the sense of wellbeing that comes from accomplishing its goal, the 8 is always climbing upward – but not blindly so. The 8 doesn't win by luck alone; it uses its strategic mind and determined spirit to come out on top.

Even in those rare times that the 8 finds itself down on its luck, it maintains its fortitude. The 8 knows how capable it is and has confidence that things will turn out right in the end. Willing to put in whatever effort it takes and shoulder whatever struggles are necessary to succeed, the 8 does not doubt that prosperity awaits, because it has manifested that prosperity personally.

Others naturally flock to and follow the successful 8, who more often than not finds itself in leadership roles. Unsurprisingly, this can go to the 8's head and turn them from authoritative to authoritarian. The 8 must be careful not to grow power-hungry lest it lose the support of its followers. So used to getting its way, the 8 may take their leadership for granted and come off as entitled.

Importantly, the 8 symbolizes balance – it is the infinity symbol turned on its head, two equal halves connected in a cycle. At its best, the 8 gives back to the universe with every success it makes, balancing its achievements with humility and gratitude, thus allowing the karmic cycle of prosperity to continue. But in practice, the 8 is in danger of falling terribly out of balance when success breeds greed and materialism. The 8 must continually strive toward generosity and *spiritual* wealth if it wishes to avoid these pitfalls.

9: The Humanitarian

Wisdom, awakening, completion, self-sacrifice.

The 9 holds the energy of completion, but this is not the end – it is closure in a cyclical sense. The 9 is the end of one cycle, and in it lies the potential for another. It ushers in the new through transformation, guiding us with its wisdom; after all, having been through the cycle before, the 9 has tremendous experience.

A true humanitarian, the 9 rises from its hardships and strife with renewed purpose and focuses its energy on promoting the greater good. Its firsthand experience imparts on the 9 a tremendous level of empathy. Leading by example, the 9 teaches us to navigate our hardships with grace and to come out inspired to help others by our experiences.

It sees the infinite shades of gray between black and white; it does not draw lines or put people into boxes but respects everyone, from the humblest of creatures to mighty kings. The energy of the 9 can awaken us to our higher selves, as it contains deep and well-rounded spiritual wisdom.

Like the 6, its upside-down twin, the 9 is very supportive and caring to the point of self-sacrifice. It tends to attract others to it and sees itself as a fixer. The

9 is a great source of advice, healing, and comfort during troubling times.

But with all it puts itself through for others, the 9 is in danger of building resentment if it doesn't allow itself space to process its feelings and heal its wounds. The 9 is prone to the mindset that 'life is suffering' and can even find comfort in its own misery; the more it sees hardship as its personal cross to bear, the more hardship it welcomes onto its path.

DIVINE PURPOSE: THE MASTER NUMBERS

Earlier we learned how to reduce any word or number to a single digit, and I told you that there were a few exceptions to this rule in numerology. Enter the master numbers: 11, 22, and 33. These numbers contain so much power and potential that numerologists leave them in their double-digit form where they show up in an individual's numerological chart – but only if that master number is one of your core numbers or found in one of your period or pinnacle cycles, which we'll discuss later.

Why do these master numbers hold such influence? All numbers with repeating digits are more powerful than other numbers: 22, 33, 44, 55, etc., are examples of what numerologists call power numbers, which amplify the qualities of their corresponding single-digit number (e.g., the 88 is twice as successful as the 8). The 11, 22, and 33 are special not only because they contain repeated digits, but because those repeated digits are the 1, 2, and 3, respectively. The true power of the master numbers lies in their sum: the 11, in addition to amplified qualities of the 1, takes on the intuitive qualities of the 2, and so on.

Karmically, those born under a master number have learned the lessons of numbers 1-9 in previous lifetimes; they are reborn here on earth to use their wisdom to improve humanity. These numbers have a divine purpose, and those who are born under them are destined to make the world a better place.

There is an elegant story of spiritual growth found in what is called the "triangle of enlightenment." This is the sequential nature of the master numbers. The difference between 11 and 22 is the same as the distance between 22 and 33, which is 11. This reveals to us that to move beyond spiritual enlightenment (11: the master dreamer) to apply our dreams in the real world (22: the master-builder), we need an even greater, more rounded spiritual experience (11+11). Likewise, when we travel through enlightenment again (11+11+11), we find the ability to pass on this spiritual and earthly mastering of things to others (33: the master teacher).

When a master number shows up in your chart, it indicates incredible potential, but it is up to *you* to harness this energy. There are dark sides to the master numbers, and with great power comes great responsibility.

11: The Master Dreamer

Intuition, illumination, potential, anxiety.

The number of spiritual enlightenment, sacred to psychics, 11 is all about illumination – a seer. It pushes the boundaries of human experience to unheard of spiritual heights. The 11 is the channel between the mortal and immortal, the human and the spirit realms.

This master number has an uncanny awareness and deep understanding of things others simply cannot see. Sensitive to subtle shifts in energy, this intuition can be both a blessing and a curse. Having such a clear vision of the full reality of the universe can be quite overwhelming and can create anxiety.

The 11 has all the characteristics of the 2 – especially intuition in droves – but it balances these qualities with its two 1s, a double dose of willpower and charisma. Thus, within the 11 is a powerful duality, a warrior god and a fertility goddess in one. With all these intense blessings, the 11 walks a fine line between unparalleled greatness and complete self-destruction.

Truly a dreamer, the 11 listens to its heart over its head every time – not the most practical of numbers by far. The 11 lives such a spiritually rich life that it simply doesn't have the capacity for advancements on the physical plane. Its head is in the clouds. While the 11 has immense potential for spiritual enlightenment, manifestation in the material world just isn't 11's game; leave that to master builder 22.

22: The Master Builder

Power, materialization, foundations, pressure.

22 is double 11, and so it is blessed with the same intuition with the added gifts of practicality and real-world effort from its sum, 4. The true essence of the 22 is its ability to experience all that the 11 has to offer in spiritual enlightenment and then actually apply it in the material realm.

This is what makes 22 the master builder, capable of materializing grand ideas into reality and destined to do so for the betterment of mankind. Its potential for success is unmatched, making the 22 possibly the most powerful number in all of numerology.

Like the 4, the 22 is highly pragmatic and builds on a strong foundation of rational thought, but the 22 has much stronger people skills and keen instincts from its double-whammy of 2s. This makes the 22 an incredibly powerful force for actualization, dedicating Herculean effort to make something of real value, with the greater purpose of life never far from their mind.

The downside to all this potential for greatness is the capacity to waste it, and the 22 is highly susceptible to the "pressure-cooker effect," pushing themselves hard to succeed and bottling up all that pressure until it finally explodes. Alternatively, if you fail to harness the power of the 22 where it appears in your chart, you may find yourself idling with no accomplishments to show for yourself. Accept your fate and rise to the occasion, and nothing can stop you.

33: The Master Teacher

Compassion, understanding, responsibility, suffering.

The rarest number in numerology, the 33 won't come up in many charts and is especially uncommon as a life path number. It is the embodiment of pure light and unconditional love, radiating warmth to everyone it touches. It is a conduit for divine guidance here on earth, and it has the great responsibility to teach others about healing, enlightenment, and betterment. The 33 is steadfastly, selflessly dedicated to this cause.

The 33 amplifies the 3's power of expression and adds to it the energy of the ultimate caregiver, the 6. You can see how a mastery of communication combined with a deep desire to help and heal others makes this number the "master teacher."

Combining the 11 and the 22, the 33 boosts this master energy to another level. It represents the culmination of all self-improvement endeavors, the most spiritually evolved number, the pinnacle of the "triangle of enlightenment."

The 33 is destined to a life of hardship and heartache, and if you have this master number in your chart, you must learn to overcome adversity with grace. It is this first-hand experience, which can feel quite harrowing, that gives the 33 its immense compassion and ability to deeply understand others.

2

HOW YOUR BIRTHDAY
INFLUENCES YOUR LIFE

E nough with the definitions and history lessons – it's time for you to start calculating your own numerological chart, to harness the power of this ancient practice to reach your fullest potential!

We'll begin with the core numbers, two of which, the life path number and the birthday number, are calculated using your date of birth.

It is not by chance that you were born on a specific day, month, and year: your birth date has a unique, powerful vibration. Numerologists believe that the date of our birth aligns with cosmic forces that help us embody the best of ourselves.

LIFE PATH NUMBER

Arguably the most influential number in your numerological chart, your life path number is the perfect place to start when calculating your core numbers. Much like the sun sign in astrology, your life path number tells you about your core self and your individual strengths and weaknesses, but it goes a step further to reveal your true purpose.

Put simply, this number represents the road you travel in life, revealing the opportunities and challenges you'll find along the way. From your life path number, you can glean the lessons you are meant to learn in this lifetime.

Calculating Your Life Path Number

First, use addition to find the single-digit sum of your date of birth and separately sum the digits of the numerical month and year of your birth, like so:

$$December\ 14,\ 1979$$
$$December = 12 = 1 + 2 = 3$$
$$14 = 1 + 4 = 5$$
$$1979 = 1 + 9 + 7 + 9 = 26 = 2 + 6 = 8$$

Use the numerical equivalent for the month of your birth; do not use a cipher to translate the letters to numbers. December is obviously represented here by the number 12 because it is the 12th month of the year.

Next, add these three sums together, again using addition to reach a single-digit sum – unless you end up with master numbers 11, 22, or 33, which you will not reduce. This root number is your life path number.

$$3 + 5 + 8 = 16 = 1 + 6 = 7$$

So, an individual born on December 14, 1979 has a life path number of 7. Another example:

January 4, 1995
January = 1
$4 = 4$
$1995 = 1 + 9 + 9 + 5 = 24 = 2 + 4 = 6$
$1 + 4 + 6 = 11$

Because 11 is a master number, and because we are calculating one of the core numbers in a numerological chart, we stop here and do not further reduce the 11.

Now, you try it! In a notebook, let's begin creating your chart. Calculate your life path number using the method above and write it down in your notebook. Read on to discover the path that awaits you.

Life Path 1

You are a natural leader, commanding respect and attention. You prefer to take charge rather than take a supporting role, and thrive in the limelight. You're ready and eager to assume responsibility for your loved ones. On the other hand, you may be quick to anger when you don't get your way, as your leadership potential comes along with the potential for a controlling nature.

You have the determination and drive you need to get results: once you commit to a goal, there is no stopping you from achieving it. In business, you make an excellent owner or entrepreneur – any position in which you can be your own boss. You are destined to find success in whatever you do in life, as long as you apply your drive appropriately.

Tending toward undue criticism of both yourself and others, take care that you don't become too concerned with appearances.

Life Path 2

You are a highly sensitive person; a quality that is both a strength and a weakness, depending on how you harness it. You experience life on a deeper level than others, but with this gift comes a tendency to hold back for fear of breaking the peace.

You are keenly in tune with the feelings of others, possessing considerable empathy and compassion. The mediator of the group, you help keep everyone together and projects moving forward harmoniously. While you avoid the limelight, you're a powerful behind-the-scenes player.

An attentive friend and lover, people are drawn to you and your peaceful ways. But beware: your sensitivity makes for an easily bruised ego. You will build resentment if you continuously run from conflict; instead, take the inherent risk of being vulnerable with others. The rewards are numerous.

Life Path 3

You are the life of the party! A social butterfly, you make new friends everywhere you go and love to be the center of attention. Your sunny demeanor inspires the people you meet, and in the face of obstacles, your unflappable optimism prevails.

Your life path is all about expression and creativity, and you were likely born with some kind of artistic talent, be it visual, musical, or some other type. To hone the gift of self-expression, you must commit to disciplined study. Practice your skills, or you risk wasting your talents. Watch out for a tendency toward disorganization, which may lead you to be irresponsible with both your skills and your money.

To maintain that bright attitude, you may hide your sensitivity from others, covering up your pain with laughter and jokes. You must learn to let yourself be vulnerable; resist withdrawing from others, and do not hide your true feelings.

Life Path 4

Dedicated, diligent, and practical, you are a "salt of the earth" type of person, feet planted firmly on the ground. You likely have strong convictions about right and wrong, and you respect order.

Destined for success only after putting in a great deal of hard work to achieve it, you show a level of dedication far above those around you. As such, you should take care not to come off as bossy or judgmental.

Precise and methodical to the point of being overly cautious, you are good with money and tend to be financially stable, but the downside of this stability can be a resistance to change. Work to cultivate some flexibility: if you are too stubborn to embrace change, you'll surely miss out on many of life's greatest opportunities.

Life Path 5

A lover of travel and a born adventurer, you are destined to journey through life meeting many people and seeing many amazing things. With such a breadth of life experience, you are likely to be open-minded and understanding of folks from all walks of life. You value freedom above nearly all else.

You are a rarity in that you actually *like* change; a master of adaptability, you gracefully roll with the punches.

The dark side of this life path is that your love of freedom can cause a fear of commitment in both personal relationships and in work. Discipline and order are not your strong suits, and if unchecked, your zest for life may lead to addiction issues. You must cultivate focus and commitment in your endeavors.

Life Path 6

A born caretaker, you are endowed with a wealth of compassion for your fellow human. You live a life of service, and you're the one who others turn to for a shoulder to cry on. You dutifully take on the responsibility of caring for those you love, which can at times make you feel overburdened. One of your biggest challenges on this life path is learning to say "no."

Others may adore and admire you, but you remain humble. Generous and kind, charismatic and charming, you make a great friend and romantic partner. This charm of yours combined with your genuine nature means that you are quite adept at business endeavors.

One risk you take with this life path number is attracting toxic partners who could take advantage of you, abusing your love. Pay close mind to who you choose to spend your time with – not everyone is worthy of the immense love you have to give.

Life Path 7

You are the seeker, a deeply spiritual individual on a lifelong quest to answer the mysteries of life – but you balance your spirituality with rationality. With one foot firmly planted on the ground, you are capable of superior analytical thought and excel at solving puzzles and finding solutions.

You prefer to work alone without interruptions to your thoughts. Autonomy and privacy are paramount in your life, which may lead to difficulties fostering and maintaining intimacy.

You guard your rich inner life protectively, but be careful not to withdraw entirely and become isolated. If you do, you'll experience loneliness and resentment.

Nourish your relationships, and you will live up to your full potential.

Life Path 8

You are positively destined for success! A born leader, you have a talent for management in both the workplace and in the personal realm. This life path has set you up for tremendous material prosperity, but this reward comes with great risk.

Your challenge in life is to understand that the real value of money and goods lies in sharing with those less fortunate. To put it more simply: you must learn to use your powers for good rather than evil, resisting greed and temptation.

With your keen sense of style and tastes that lean toward the extravagant, you may be prone to living beyond your means, overspending as you anticipate successes that have yet to roll in. But when someone's in a pinch, there's no better friend to have than you; at your best, your generosity and goodwill touch everyone around you.

Life Path 9

You possess a deep and true love for the world, embodying the principles of humanitarianism and philanthropy. Because you find satisfaction and fulfillment in making the world a better place, you will sacrifice time, money, and energy for the greater good, doing everything within your power to better the lives of others.

Not one to pass judgment on others, you attract individuals from all walks of life with your magnetic personality. Alongside your egalitarian ideals, your life path imparts creativity, imagination, and the gift of being able to see the good in everyone and the beauty in everything.

You may quickly become disappointed when the world doesn't line up with your rosy expectations. As an idealist, you're prone to this kind of frustration. Take some time to rest and appreciate what you *have* accomplished before pushing yourself and the rest of the world to do more and be better. Progress doesn't happen overnight.

Life Path 11

With a life path of master number 11, the master dreamer, your journey in life holds incredible potential but comes with elevated challenges.

A highly intuitive person, insight comes naturally. You have supercharged psychic energy, which flows through you and out into the world, making you an inspiration to others. You must learn to harness this power, lest it cause you emotional turmoil.

You have the destiny to be a peacemaker in the world, bringing healing to others with your divine intuitive gifts. In fact, the true power of your intuition lies in your potential to serve as a channel between the earthly and spiritual realms.

But this power is a double-edged sword; you tend to be self-critical, prone to paralysis as a result of self-doubt, depression, and a lack of confidence. Finding and maintaining your confidence is the number one key to unlocking the true potential of this master number life path.

Life Path 22

With a life path of master number 22, the master builder, your journey in life holds incredible potential but comes with elevated challenges.

You are destined to make something very special during your time on this earth. You have an incredible inner vision, high ideals, and a strong conviction to make things happen – but this power is somewhat delicate. To harness it fully, you need to accept the duality of 22 when your idealism disagrees with your pragmatism.

The greatest challenge in this life path is to learn to be both a big-picture person *and* a fine details person, a visionary *and* a manager. Keeping one foot on the ground and the other in the spiritual realm will allow you to harness the power within.

You may find yourself losing out on personal relationships in pursuit of your higher purpose, with a tendency to focus on work to the detriment of all else. Mind yourself that you do not become controlling or manipulative with others, and remember the greater good of all for which you strive.

Life Path 33

A life path of 33 is exceedingly rare; only a few birthdays result in this number. If this is you, your journey in life holds incredible potential but comes with elevated challenges.

Your divine potential lies in your ability to guide others. You have access to a breadth of spiritual knowledge and the intuition necessary to tap into it. Divinely destined to share your spiritual understandings, you are adept at introspection and insightfulness.

From this keen intuition springs sincerity and immense compassion for others. Your caring nature may lead you to take on responsibilities that perhaps you should not. A major challenge of this life path is finding the balance between giving of yourself and becoming a doormat.

You may find yourself attracted to damaged, toxic individuals, who are determined to use your gifts to heal or fix them. As such, you risk finding yourself in abusive situations with people who will take advantage of your remarkably generous spirit.

BIRTHDAY NUMBER

Just as the life path number is equivalent to the astrological sun sign, the birthday number (also called the day of birth number) is like the moon sign: it represents a core part of our nature we develop early in life. The birthday number describes the talents and particular abilities a person has brought into this life – in other words, your birthday gift to the world.

The birthday number also tells us a little about how we see ourselves, and these gifts describe some of our best features. You may feel a stronger connection to your birthday number than to the description of your life path – and your close friends would probably describe you the same way.

Calculating Your Birthday Number

Your birthday number is simply the day of the month on which you were born. This is another case in which numerologists do not reduce a number through natural addition; double-digit numbers have their own meanings when it comes to the birthday number.

Make sure you write your birthday number in the notebook where you put your life path number, so we can begin building your numerological chart.

Your Unique Gift: What Your Birthday Number Says About You

1. You are an innovative self-starter, and with a powerful determination of will, you can conquer any challenge you may face. You're never afraid to be the first at something, you love to try new things.
2. Your intuition and empathy endow you with a great deal of compassion. You remain unbiased, able to see all sides of the situation, which makes you a natural mediator and influential person.
3. An excellent communicator and charming conversationalist, your bright personality inspires everyone around you. Naturally

creative, you likely have a talent for some form of art or self-expression.

4. Ruled by rationality and pragmatism, you work hard and persevere. You are a dependable friend, and people are often attracted to your down-to-earth ways.

5. Most people dislike change, but you're an exception. Super adaptable, you thrive in dynamic environments, energized by the excitement.

6. A born nurturer, your gift to the world is your love. With a big heart, you have a strong drive to heal and comfort others, and you're fiercely protective of those under your care.

7. With a keen mind, you have one foot on the ground and one in the spiritual realm. Your gift is your curiosity, and you will learn much in your lifetime.

8. You are destined for success! With the capability to match your ambition, your gift is that you can reach any goal you set.

9. You have a heart of gold and are truly altruistic, finding meaning in life through helping others. You are destined to change the world for the better.

10. With a sharp mind, your gift is that you not only can envision brilliant new solutions, but

you have the skill to organize all the details necessary and carry your plans to completion.

11. You have keen skills of perception and the gift of great insight. Your powerful intuition helps you understand and guide others.

12. Your gifts are those of creativity and imagination. You are unafraid to be unique, and people are drawn to your bright personality and trueness to yourself.

13. You are both an optimist and highly practical. Hardworking, you stay on track toward reaching your high ideals.

14. Your gift is your open mind. You love to try new things, but you are also blessed with pragmatism, which will take you far in life.

15. A social butterfly, you will meet many people in your life. With a deep capacity to love, you'll touch everyone you meet with your gift of warmth.

16. You possess an inquisitive mind, always seeking the truth. Your wisdom is your gift to the world.

17. Highly independent and self-motivated, you prefer to work alone, and you can accomplish amazing things when left to your own devices.

18. While you may be shy and quiet, your true gift is your capacity for service to others. You are

destined to leave the world better than you found it.

19. With unparalleled courage, you take risks and earn rewards that bring great things into your life, and are capable of accomplishing anything.

20. Your gift is an ability to relate to others on a deep, cosmic level. Relationships are harmonious and cooperative when you are involved.

21. An extrovert, you thrive in social situations, finding fulfillment in connecting with others. Plenty of natural charm is your gift, and people are drawn to you.

22. You are destined to make something great. You are a hard worker and a great team player.

23. Your gift to others is your optimism; with your zest for life, you inspire those you meet. You enjoy adventure and have an easygoing outlook on life.

24. You are a nurturer and provider, and you maintain healthy, balanced relationships. Your gift to the world is your loyal heart.

25. **25:** A curious person, you observe everything around you, taking in and processing much information. Your gift to the world is your thirst for knowledge, which will take you to great places.

26. You have a strong drive to succeed, but you feel most fulfilled when your work benefits others, not only yourself. You have the intuitive gift of knowing what people want.

27. Compassionate and tolerant, you have a gift for absorbing huge amounts of knowledge, and you are destined to use it for the greater good.

28. You understand the value of working as a team. Your gift in life is your natural leadership; you push your team to succeed.

29. You have a gift for bringing people together, using intuition to see the connection between everything and everyone.

30. A great thinker, your creative ideas are your gift to the world, and they are destined to uplift others.

31. You take a balanced approach in life. Relying on both practicality and imagination, your dual gifts are creativity and the organizational skills necessary to manifest your dreams.

3

UNCOVERING THE SECRETS OF YOUR NAME

So, now you've learned how to calculate two of the five core numbers in your numerological chart, based on your date of birth. Next, you'll discover the divine secrets behind your name as we uncover the three remaining core numbers: your expression number, personality number, and soul urge number.

In addition, we'll reveal a sixth number from your name that numerologists don't count as part of your core –your hidden passion number, which can reveal a great deal about you.

EXPRESSION NUMBER

While your life path number helps uncover the lessons you are meant to learn in this lifetime, your expression number reveals *how* you will accomplish what you set out to do on your life path. This is why it is sometimes called the destiny number. It tells you about the talents and shortcomings you brought with you into this life and, along with your life path number, is one of the most influential numbers in your chart.

Calculating Your Expression Number

Remember the chart from Chapter One, based on the Pythagorean numerological alphabet:

1	2	3	4	5	6	7	8	9
A	B	C	D	E	F	G	H	I
J	K	L	M	N	O	P	Q	R
S	T	U	V	W	X	Y	Z	

Use this cipher to "translate" your name from letters into numbers. You should use your full name, including first, middle, and last, though you can choose whether to use your married or birth name. (More on that later in the chapter.)

Sum each name individually until you reach a single-digit number (or an 11, 22, or 33). Finally, add all individual name sums together and reduce as necessary to reach either a single digit or a master number.

For example:

$$DELPHINA = 4+5+3+7+8+9+5+1 = 42 = 4+$$
$$2 = 6$$
$$MARIE = 4+1+9+9+5 = 28 = 2+8 = 10 = 1+0 = 1$$
$$WOODS = 5+6+6+4+1 = 22$$
$$Delphina\ Marie\ Woods = 6+1+22 = 29 = 2+9 = 11$$

It's quite simple, really! Notice that when I encountered a master number, I stopped adding.

Let's see an example of a name that looks a little different. In the case below, "Jean-Claude" is the actor's full first name, and "van Damme" is a two-word surname, so the calculation looks like this:

$$JEANCLAUDE = 1+5+1+5+3+3+1+3+4+5 =$$
$$31 = 3+1 = 4$$
$$VANDAMME = 4+1+5+4+1+4+4 = 23 = 2+$$
$$3 = 5$$
$$Jean\text{-}Claude\ van\ Damme = 4+5 = 9$$

Your turn. In the notebook where we're creating your chart, calculate your expression number using the method above. Now read on to unveil your destiny.

What Destiny Does Your Expression Number Hold?

Expression 1

A natural-born leader with a knack for making your own opportunities, you bravely venture where others dare not tread – and you make the journey look easy! Extremely self-sufficient, you are at your most productive and innovative when you go it alone.

You may struggle, though, to cooperate with others, finding that you lack the patience for their thoughts and opinions. Your loved ones may see you as aggressive or self-centered, and you'd do well to practice thinking before you speak.

Expression 2

Cooperative and supportive by nature, you shine when working with others. Always striving for balance, you make a great partner in relationships of all kinds. Your intuition enables you to read people and situations so you can react with compassion. Your loved ones see you as humble and gentle but with strength of will.

The downside of this is that you are prone to having your feelings hurt, and you tend toward self-doubt when making decisions on your own. Try following your head instead of your heart more often and see where it takes you.

Expression 3

You have a real way with words, able to elegantly convey creative ideas and inspire those around you – communication comes so naturally to you! People are drawn to your magnetic charm, and they stay for your unparalleled optimism, which means you have a broad social circle.

On the flip side, you tend to be rather shallow – both in your relationships and in the rest of your life. You have difficulty committing to any one person or situation long enough to delve deeply, and a healthy dose of self-discipline would do you well.

Expression 4

A master of project management, your hardworking and highly organized nature means that others trust you to follow through on your word. You are down-to-earth and highly capable at whatever you put your mind to, patient, honest, and loyal – maybe even to a fault.

Set firmly in your ways, you are known for being stubborn, and your determination may lead you to ignore innovative ways of thinking. The greatest challenge for those with the expression number 4 is learning to let go.

Expression 5

An adventurous soul, you crave freedom and want to experience everything the world has to offer. Your many passions carry you forward, and because your interests take you so many places, you've learned to adapt to your surroundings.

However, all this change breeds inconsistency, especially when your passions turn out to be temporary flights of fancy. Others may see you as unreliable.

Expression 6

Your greatest gift is in how you relate to others. You are fiercely loyal and protective of those you love, especially your family. With a nurturing soul and a heart of gold, you live to support and uplift those in need.

Your challenge is to put yourself first and practice self-care. You can't heal others when your own body, mind, and spirit are not in top shape. You may find that abusive individuals are drawn to your giving nature.

Expression 7

Driven by a great desire for knowledge and wisdom, you are ready and eager to dive deep into both the spiritual and intellectual realms in search of truths. Highly logical and analytical, you have everything you need to make the most of the knowledge you gain.

The downside is that you may struggle to relate to other people, who might find your esoteric ways off-putting. You tend towards being suspicious of others and thus isolate yourself, because you look for problems where there are none.

Expression 8

With lucky number 8 for an expression number, you are blessed with good judgment and great business sense. Highly resourceful and ambitious, you achieve every goal you set your mind to and are destined for material success.

But ambition is a double-edged sword, and you are in danger of letting your leadership skills turn into authoritarian demands. Take care to strive for more than just material goods; the people around you are worth more than their weight in gold.

Expression 9

Blessed with tremendous compassion, you find the good in everyone and in every situation. You strive to better the lives of others on both an intimate scale, by providing support for loved ones, and on a universal scale, as a philanthropist and humanitarian.

Keep focused on that altruism and your high ideals. If you give in to suffering and lose sight of the bigger picture, you'll only wallow alone in misery.

Expression 11

Driving by your instincts and divine inspiration, you have a beautiful idealistic vision for the world and a clear picture of the way things should be. A beacon of hope to those in need, your charisma attracts everyone to you.

However, you may lack the practical skills and organized mind to bring your amazing dreams to fruition. Your challenge is bringing your head down from the clouds without losing sight of that divine guidance.

Expression 22

You are destined to create something great. An adept problem-solver, capable of guiding others to make incredible things happen as a team, you make an excellent team leader when you focus on cooperation.

But because you are so driven and headstrong, you run the risk of having domination and control issues, losing the support of those around you. Remember that you are in control of your destiny but that you cannot fulfill this destiny without the help of others.

Expression 33

You possess a unique combination of strength of heart and clarity of mind. Blessed with both a powerful intuition and the communication skills to share it, you are a highly enlightened individual who sets an example for others.

While other people turn to you for help and support, you may feel burdened by all that you carry on your shoulders. The key is to give of yourself freely; use your gifts to their greatest extent, and you'll get back all that you give and more.

PERSONALITY NUMBER

This core number in your numerological chart is pretty much self-explanatory: it's all about your personality! It represents the traits and characteristics you show to the world outwardly.

In contrast to your expression number, which describes your core self, your personality number reveals how you present yourself to others and how you relate to the outside world. It also relates to your individual sense of style and how you dress. Embracing the energies of your personality number is key to practicing self-compassion and living your best life.

Calculating Your Personality Number

Numerologists contend, again based on Pythagoras's teachings (which were based on Chaldean numerological principals), that consonants represent your public, outward persona, while vowels represent your innermost feelings and beliefs. This is where the final two core numbers in your chart come into play. Your personality number is calculated using only the consonants of your full name.

To convert letters to numbers, refer back to the Pythagorean cipher from earlier in this chapter and use only the consonants in your name.

For example:

Delphina Marie Woods =
$$D L P H N = 4 + 2 + 7 + 8 + 5 = 26 = 2 + 6 = 8$$
$$M R = 4 + 9 = 13 = 1 + 3 = 4$$
$$W D S = 5 + 4 + 1 = 10 = 1 + 0 = 1$$
$$8 + 4 + 1 = 13 = 1 + 3 = 4$$

Pretty simple, right? Remember to stop reducing if you land on a master number during your calculations, since the personality number is one of your core numbers:

$$Brenda\ Cox =$$
$$B\ R\ N\ D = 2 + 9 + 5 + 4 = 20 = 2 + 0 = 2$$
$$C\ X = 3 + 6 = 9$$
$$2 + 9 = 11$$

As for the ever-adaptable letter Y, when calculating your personality number, only include Ys in your name that serve as consonants; where a Y is used as a vowel, ignore it. For example:

$$Yancy = Y\ N\ C = 7 + 5 + 3 = 15 = 1 + 5 = 6$$

We counted the first Y because it has the hard sound of a consonant, but we did not count the Y at the end because this one acts as a vowel.

Ready to give it a go? Calculate your personality number using this method. Write down the number in your chart that we're building in your notebook, and read on to explore your outward traits!

Embrace Yourself: What Your Personality Number Says About You

Personality 1

Fearless and always at the forefront, you're a natural leader. You're great at managing people to help a team complete challenging projects, and your perseverance inspires those around you. People find you quite likable. You dress to impress and leave a dignified impression.

Personality 2

Reliable and fair, tranquil and trustworthy, you make a great peacemaker and mediator. Your sensitive nature makes you a good listener, and anyone would be lucky to have you as a companion. Because relationships are paramount to you, you are particularly conscientious with your appearance.

Personality 3

Artistic and creative, you have an exceptional way of expressing yourself. You're a real charmer and great conversationalist, and people gravitate to you because you give love and affection easily. Style-wise, you love jewelry and glitz and glam, never missing an opportunity to dress up.

Personality 4

Hardworking and dependable, you are highly devoted to your community and family. You have amazing strength of character. You tend toward the practical in both thought and your personal style, often choosing comfort over fashion.

Personality 5

You're the adventurous type, always seeking out new things, and are highly adaptable to change. You have an unforgettable presence, and others love to have conversations with you about your many life experiences. Your enthusiasm is infectious. When it comes to style, you are always on-trend.

Personality 6

Highly compassionate, you find your fulfillment in the roles of nurturer or protector. Your loving disposition and depth of sympathy make you an excellent compatriot. People look to you for comfort in times of great strife. Not particularly concerned with fashion, you prefer to dress casually.

Personality 7

A bit of an outsider, your highly philosophical mind can make you seem enigmatic or aloof, but once others get to know you, they find that you're a genuine and kind person. You're insatiably curious and love to discover what makes things tick. You either pay no mind to fashion or prefer classic or vintage styles.

Personality 8

A person of great influence, you have a powerful presence and excel in executive leadership positions. Couple your dedication with your enthusiasm and optimism, and you've got a recipe for success! When it comes to your fashion sense, only the well-made or bespoke will do.

Personality 9

Generous and kind, understanding and trustworthy, people flock to you for advice and wisdom. You wear your heart on your sleeve and have a deep connection to your spirituality. You probably look younger than your age.

Personality 11

You are very in touch with your intuition and have a rich inner life. Deeply spiritual, your energy is healing to others, and you radiate wellness. Not one to compromise your morals for fashion, you strive to wear ethical clothing above all else.

Personality 22

Never afraid to get your hands dirty, you're both a hard worker and a great leader who knows how to delegate – your communication skills shine! Your grounded, practical nature, combined with your generosity of spirit, makes you quite popular with others. As for clothing, style comes second to you after performance and durability.

Personality 33

You inspire confidence in those around you and are a natural teacher, excellent at clearly communicating abstract ideas. You are very giving of yourself, and that generosity draws abundance to you. You have a chic, effortless style.

SOUL URGE NUMBER

The soul urge number reveals your innermost, private desires and sense of self – similar to the moon sign in astrology. It is sometimes called the heart's desire number. It is the guiding force that brought you into this life, and it is reflected in your innermost wishes, as well as your darkest fears.

Harnessing the power of your soul urge number can be deeply healing. Many report improvements in their mental health upon discovering their soul urge number and learning of their truest motivations in life.

Calculating Your Soul Urge Number

Based on what you learned about the personality number, can you guess how the soul urge number is calculated? If you guessed "vowels," you're spot-on. Just like with your personality number, you'll find your soul urge number by taking a closer look at your name and removing those letters that apply only to your outer personality, the consonants. Refer back to the cipher.

Again, my name, for example:

$$Delphina\ Marie\ Woods =$$
$$E\ I\ A = 5 + 9 + 1 = 15 = 1 + 5 = 6$$
$$A\ I\ E = 1 + 9 + 5 = 15 = 1 + 5 = 6$$
$$O\ O = 6 + 6 = 12 = 1 + 2 = 3$$
$$6 + 6 + 3 = 15 = 1 + 5 = 6$$

Don't forget to stop reducing if you hit a master number, because we are calculating a core number here:

$$Glover =$$
$$O\ E = 6 + 5 = 11$$

You will only include the letter Y or the number 7 in your calculation for the soul urge number if the Y is used as a vowel. For example, with the name Emily, we count the Y at the end:

$$Emily = E\ I\ Y = 5 + 9 + 7 = 21 = 2 + 1 = 3$$

However, in the case of the name Yancy, the first Y behaves like a consonant, so it is not used when calculating the soul urge number. Only the second Y is counted:

$$Yancy = A\ Y = 1 + 7 = 8$$

Your turn. Calculate your soul urge number and write it down in your chart in your notebook. Now let's uncover your truest desires.

Fun fact: an easier way to get your soul urge number is to subtract your personality number from your expression number – and the opposite works as well to find your personality number. Just the elegant magic of numerology at work. Try both methods for yourself and see!

Your Heart's Desire: What Your Soul Urge Number Reveals

Soul Urge 1

Your soul urge is a driving force! You trust your instincts above all else. You are convinced that your actions have great meaning in the world, and you are correct. You have a deep need to be heard and will *only* feel fulfilled in leadership roles, where your natural abilities and pioneering spirit will thrive.

With the kind of self-assurance you possess, you might have run-ins with authority figures throughout your life. You tend towards dominance and should be careful not to silence others – you're the type of person who doesn't even notice when you've hurt someone's feelings. When it comes down to it, though, you are incredibly loyal, and you'll receive loyalty in return.

Soul Urge 2

Your heart's desire is to be not just loved but needed. You have a deep desire to connect with others on a personal level and strive toward balance and cooperation in all your relationships. You're a natural team player and will only thrive when you are part of something larger than yourself.

You're skilled at cooperation and keeping the peace – which is great for you because interpersonal conflict is *not* something you handle well. Your need to be loved leads to a sensitivity that can make uncomfortable situations deeply troubling for you. You're also prone to distrusting yourself because you so highly value the consensus of others. The truth is, your strength in interpersonal relationships comes from your strong intuition, so you must learn to trust your gut.

Soul Urge 3

Your soul urge is to create; above all, you need to express yourself. You're great at it, too – inspiring and original, artistic and brilliant, you have everything within you necessary to be successful as a creative. The way you share your deepest self so freely and openly through communication draws others to you like a magnet, and your positivity is infectious.

The downside is that you're likely to be disorganized, scattered in your thoughts and endeavors. You'll never be satisfied until you create your masterpiece, so you'd do well to cultivate better focus. Narrow in on one of your many passions and pursue it until the end, no matter what critics may say.

Soul Urge 4

Your deepest need is to find stability and order amongst life's chaos. Practicality and reliability are your greatest virtues, and these traits lend themselves well to domestic endeavors. You excel at organizing the world around you, making not just sense but usefulness out of whatever comes your way. Loyal and generous, people are drawn to you, and you are a natural project manager.

On the flip side, your down-to-earth realism and honesty mean that you can come across as unkind and tactless, and your need for stability makes you disastrously resistant to change. You should work to cultivate a zen-like attitude so you can keep the solid foundation you need no matter the upheaval you may find yourself in.

Soul Urge 5

Your heart's desire is to experience everything you can in this lifetime. Your thirst for adventure and curiosity of mind means that you're only satisfied when you're on a quest – for you, it's all about the journey, not the destination. You only feel alive when you're in motion, and this enthusiasm is inspirational to others.

You'll make many friends on your journey through life, but maintaining friendships is your challenge, as you are always onto the next thing, leaving others behind. Your fear of commitment is your downfall; you must learn to dig deeper and stick around when the going gets tough.

Soul Urge 6

Your deepest desire is to nurture and care for those you love. You have a gift for helping others thrive and flourish, and an intuitive sense of what others need. You find fulfillment when you can see tangible results of your influence in the lives of your loved ones – you're only happy when they're happy!

But this kind of selflessness can easily lead you to ignore your own needs in favor of the needs of others. Remember you have to put on your own oxygen mask before you can help someone else put on theirs. If you don't have oxygen, you're of no use to anyone, which is why you must put yourself first in order to give your best to others.

Soul Urge 7

Your soul is compelled by the pursuit of knowledge. You're on an endless quest to answer life's greatest mysteries, both intellectual and spiritual, and you won't be satisfied until you have uncovered profound truths, building your own wisdom along the way.

You likely feel as if you don't belong around others. Interpersonal communication doesn't come naturally to you, and others see you as reclusive or enigmatic. This leads to painful isolation. Remember that without anyone to share your findings with, all your theories, brilliant ideas and discoveries will go to waste.

Soul Urge 8

Your soul urge is for prosperity and status. You're highly motivated by achievement, especially when your successes come with a financial reward. However, you will never find fulfillment unless you learn the value of sharing your material wealth with others for the greater good of the world. You must be altruistic and avoid the trap of selfishness.

Confident and ambitious, you're a natural leader and have everything within you to reach the levels of success you so desire. But your strong personality can come off as domineering – mind that you don't hurt anyone on your climb to the top, as you'll need people behind you to support you in your journey.

Soul Urge 9

Your pure heart desires nothing more or less than to make the world a better place. A humanitarian at heart, you only want the best for others and possess the rare gifts of profound empathy and wisdom. Altruism is your highest ideal, and you will find fulfillment by leaving a lasting legacy of love on this earth.

An idealist and optimist, you always see the silver lining. The downside to this perspective is that the faith you have in others is not always warranted; you believe everyone shares the same ideals as you. In fact, you are in danger of being taken advantage of, forever giving of yourself to those who do not deserve it.

Soul Urge 11

Your heart's desire is to trust your inner voice. A remarkably intuitive, sensitive soul, you likely have psychic gifts that may manifest in dreams or simply as insights you cannot explain. You are drawn to embark on a spiritual journey, but you'll only be complete when you look inside yourself – you won't find the answers in others' teachings.

Your keen empathy is a wonderful gift that draws people to you, but being so aware of what others think and feel also makes you prone to anxiousness. You might feel ungrounded as you move through life exposed to other people's emotions, and learning to harness your ability to channel energy between the material and spiritual realms will be difficult with all these distractions.

Soul Urge 22

Your soul urge is a grand one: you must find a way in this lifetime to transform the world. Your visionary eye makes you an architect of the future, not just for yourself but for others, and in your heart, you dream of building a utopia. Fortunately, you have the grounded mind and practical skills to make your dreams a reality.

You inspire in others a sense of stability and security, and you make a great leader or organizer. You'll only meet your true calling when you lean on others for help in pursuit of your big goals. You're destined for greatness, but you're also prone to letting all of this stagnate from the pressure you put on yourself. You must learn to accept the help of others and push through to your goals no matter the challenges in your way.

Soul Urge 33

It is exceedingly rare to have a 33 for your soul urge number. Your heart's desire is to pass on wisdom to the next generation. You're a natural teacher and will find your true happiness in life when you devote yourself to educating or healing others. You lack personal ambition in pursuit of this – it's all for the greater good.

This is an immense responsibility your soul has taken on, and you may find yourself shirking it. You may find it challenging to be a leader, but to find peace in this life, you must not resist your inner calling.

HIDDEN PASSION NUMBER

The hidden passion number is not considered one of the core numbers in your numerological chart, but nonetheless, it should not be overlooked, as it reveals much about you. Your hidden passion is a reflection of the vibrations that occur most often in your name, and it tells you about your natural talents and personal power.

Finding Your Hidden Passion

Return to your expression number calculation. This time, you're not interested in the sums. Instead, you'll count the frequency with which each number appears in your full name. For instance:

$$DELPHINA = 4 + 5 + 3 + 7 + 8 + 9 + 5 + 1$$
$$MARIE = 4 + 1 + 9 + 9 + 5$$
$$WOODS = 5 + 6 + 6 + 4 + 1$$

The vibrations in my name are three 1s, zero 2s, one 3, three 4s, four 5s, two 6s, one 7, one 8, and three 9s. With more 5s than any other number, my hidden passion is 5.

If you have six or more of any one number in your full name, this can indicate a tipping of the balance, and your hidden power can drive you to malicious characteristics.

Find your own hidden passion and record it in your chart, and read below to discover how you harness this number's power.

Your Secret Talent: What Your Hidden Passion Number Means

Hidden Passion 1

You are a warrior, a leader, and a survivor. Highly competent and energetic, you have the strength to overcome any obstacle. You would do well in politics or as a professional athlete. If you have six or more 1s in your full name, your competitive nature may make you aggressive – even violent – and the politician in you is in danger of becoming a tyrant.

Hidden Passion 2

You are the ideal team player. Considerate and insightful, you're the pillar of your organization. You are dedicated to your work in whatever you put your mind to, and people naturally come to rely on you greatly. If you have six or more 2s in your full name, your sensitivity can rise to extreme heights, making you quite thin-skinned.

Hidden Passion 3

Your hidden passion is your *talent*: you are highly creative, expressive, and artistic. You will excel in some form of art, whether visual, written, musical, or some other type. Your charm and charisma touch everyone around you, and you have a rich social life. If you have six or more 3s in your name, your creative success is likely to be seriously hindered by your scattered, superficial interests and lack of dedication.

Hidden Passion 4

You are solid as a rock and the salt of the earth. You love to work and won't be satisfied unless you are putting in hard work to accomplish something; idle time is not in your schedule. Your friends and family put great faith in you, and you never let them down. If you have six or more 4s in your full name, you must work hard to avoid a narrow-minded, rigid worldview.

Hidden Passion 5

Your hidden passion is a zest for life! You're all about traveling and taking adventures, and you embrace every new challenge. You have a way with words and a talent for learning languages. Careers that utilize writing or speaking will suit you well. If you have six or more 5s in your name, though, you lack discipline; prone to overindulgence, you can be a slave to your impulses if you're not vigilant.

Hidden Passion 6

Your hidden power is your unflappable idealism. You thrive when you apply yourself in service to others. Responsible and eager to help, you would make an excellent teacher or counselor, not to mention a great life partner and parent. But if you have six or more 6s in your full name, your high ideals and strong opinions could edge over into obnoxious self-righteousness.

Hidden Passion 7

Your secret power is your keen mind and highly developed intellect. You have no difficulty with abstract thought and would do well as a researcher. Adept at problem-solving, there is nothing you love more than finding the solution to a difficult puzzle. With six or more 7s in your name, however, you're likely to lose yourself to your studies and become isolated, melancholic, and bitter.

Hidden Passion 8

Your secret talent sets you up for great success, as you're blessed with both practical business sense and an overarching vision. You gravitate naturally toward leadership positions, and your subordinates tend to love working for you. You must be careful to avoid avarice. Don't let your success go to your head and damage your moral compass. You're especially at risk of this with multiple 8s in your name.

Hidden Passion 9

Your hidden talent is your creativity, but unlike those with a hidden passion of 3, you are unlikely to harness yours until later in life. You have a strong desire to help those in need, and your warmth and compassion give you an edge in any humanitarian work you undertake. With six or more 9s in your name, you risk leaning too hard into the abstract and failing to materialize any of your ideas.

THE NUMEROLOGY OF NAME CHANGES & NICKNAMES

You're probably wondering what happens if you change your name or go by something different than the name you were born with. Maybe you have a nickname that others call you. Maybe you go by your middle name instead of your first. It's very common for people to change their surnames when they marry or are adopted, and it's not unheard of for individuals to change their full names entirely for a variety of personal and legal reasons. Let's not forget about celebrities, who often change all or part of their name to be more memorable, or because someone else in the industry has the same birth name.

Most numerologists stress the importance of using your full birth name when calculating your core numbers. In fact, if your name happens to be misspelled on your birth certificate, some would instruct you to use the misspelled version! The idea behind this is that the energies in your name at birth are with you for the rest of your life, no matter what names you take on as you grow and change.

These birth name vibrations have an especially profound influence on your life path number, and I strongly recommend that you calculate your life path number based on your exact birth name. The personality number and soul urge number, however, are a little bit of a gray area.

The name you're known as, the way you introduce yourself, and the name your friends and loved ones call you holds a great deal of power. These are the vibrations that are repeated around you every time someone calls you by your name, every time you sign a document, every time you sign off on an email – so of course, any name change has a profound effect on your numerology.

Some numerologists recommend calculating your personality and soul urge numbers on your birth name *and also* on your current name, the latter of which are called your minor personality and minor soul urge, respectively. But for some of us, the influence of our chosen name may be much more than "minor."

Ultimately, it is up to you alone which names you use in these calculations. I suggest you try them all and consider how they each fit you to have the fullest picture of your name numerology.

Here are some characteristics of the vibrations in birth names and chosen names to help you understand how each piece of the puzzle comes together to make you, you.

Birth Name Influence	Chosen Name Influence
The blueprint for your ultimate destiny	How you approach the world
Your innate talents and gifts	How you see yourself and want to be seen
Parts of you that you hide from others	What you're comfortable expressing openly

4

KARMIC INFLUENCE – THE KEYS TO YOUR SPIRITUAL EVOLUTION

With its roots in the Kabbalah and other ancient spiritual systems, numerology deals heavily in the business of reincarnation. Numerologists believe that humans go through many iterations of life, and during each of our many lifetimes, we accumulate karma.

Karma is, put simply, spiritual cause-and-effect. Our souls carry with them wisdom from our past lives each time we are reincarnated, the goal being to evolve spiritually during each lifetime until all lessons are learned. In addition to benefits from our past lives, we also carry over old burdens – mistakes we made and poor circumstances we navigated in previous incarnations, which affect us negatively in this lifetime until we learn to conquer them.

The karmic condition of your soul can be revealed through the vibrations of numbers in your numerological chart in two principal ways: karmic lesson numbers and karmic debt numbers.

But numerology also tells us about the particular skills we are born with to conquer the adversities that come our way – through karmic influence or otherwise. Your balance number and maturity number will help you as you work through the lessons of your current lifetime.

KARMIC LESSON NUMBERS

Karmic lesson numbers are simply the missing numbers in your birth name. Those numbers that are not represented in your name show you the vibrational frequencies you're missing, or the energies you did not carry over from previous lifetimes. Thus, these missing vibrations teach us karmic lessons; they show us where we need to grow spiritually.

Do You Have Any Karmic Lesson Numbers?

It's very common to have karmic lesson numbers in your numerological chart – or more specifically, in your expression number, as we speak of karmic lessons in relation to your birth name. If you think of the energies in your birth name as tools to help you manifest in this life, karmic numbers represent the tools you don't have at your disposal. You will have to find them in this life in order to reach spiritual wholeness.

On rare occasions, an individual's full name may contain all nine of the essential vibrational frequencies that Pythagoras identified, but this does not indicate that the person is an old soul; it simply means they have all the tools they need in this life. The rest of us carry several karmic lessons, and while these may be challenging, with challenge comes opportunity.

Karmic lesson numbers are like a vacuum of vibrations ready to be filled, and their influence is reduced if they show up in your other core numbers.

To find your karmic lesson numbers (if any), recall how you calculated your expression number or destiny number in Chapter Two. Here again, you will transform the letters of your birth name into numbers, as per the Pythagorean cipher.

In this case, though, all you need to do is identify the numbers that are missing from your name. For example:

$$DELPHINA = 45378951$$
$$MARIE = 41995$$
$$WOODS = 56641$$

The number 2 is conspicuously absent from my birth name. This means that I have a karmic lesson number of 2. Thankfully, I also have a life path of 2, meaning I am driven by my intuition, and my expression number itself is 11, which sums to 2. This helps to fill the "vacuum" created by my karmic lesson.

Another example: Bill Clinton, the 42nd president of the United States, whose birth name is William Jefferson Blythe, has no karmic lesson numbers in his birth name:

$$WILLIAM = 5933914$$
$$JEFFERSON = 15665165$$
$$BLYTHE = 237285$$

Look back at your expression number calculation and determine which numbers are missing, then record your karmic lesson(s) in your chart and read on for what you can learn from them.

What Lessons Do You Have to Learn in This Life?

Karmic Lesson 1

A missing 1 indicates a lack of initiative and a dependence on others. You may struggle to find your voice among the strong-willed people in your life, but this lesson is essential to learn. You must work to be more assertive and self-confident, which will, in turn, help you overcome your tendency towards procrastination.

Karmic Lesson 2

Without the energy of the 2, you may find yourself less than tactful, struggling to work as part of a team. You must learn how to accomplish something without seeking praise or reward and strive to show more sensitivity and compassion to others. Your greatest life lesson is to cultivate patience, which will improve your relationships, both professional and personal.

Karmic Lesson 3

Your missing 3 indicates excessive self-criticism, pessimism, and a fear of failure that prevents you from truly expressing yourself. No one is perfect; you must learn to let go of the impossible standards to which you hold yourself. Otherwise, you will miss out on the greatest joys of life because you've been holding yourself back.

Karmic Lesson 4

The missing 4 is like a missing inner compass; without it, you may find yourself lost, without direction or focus. This makes you likely to seek solutions outside of yourself, and the next shiny thing always seems to be the solution... until it isn't. Your challenge is to cultivate self-discipline and concentration to build a solid foundation for your life.

Karmic Lesson 5

Rigidity and inflexibility are the hallmarks of a missing 5, and overcoming your fear of change is essential. You must broaden your horizons, welcome new opportunities, and bravely face the uncertainty of the future. This karmic lesson invites you to have faith that it will all work out in the end, to "go with the flow." You can grow and adapt, no matter how scary.

Karmic Lesson 6

A missing 6 reveals commitment issues and an inability to take responsibility in your relationships. You closely guard your heart against others to protect yourself; you likely feel isolated and lonely because the bonds you've formed are only superficial. This karmic lesson teaches you to communicate openly and honestly, and to show others vulnerability in order to cultivate healthy relationships.

Karmic Lesson 7

The karmic lesson of the 7 is to look more deeply at your life and do the work required to fully develop your mental and spiritual abilities. You tend towards only a superficial understanding of many subjects, and you must cultivate determination to perfect your talents. Otherwise, you will never reach your full potential.

Karmic Lesson 8

The missing 8 indicates financial volatility; you tend to attract money, but you let it slip through your fingers. You have a strong drive to succeed, but in pursuit of gains, you may take on too much risk. Balance is the key to this karmic lesson. Learn your limitations and make your moves more conservatively.

Karmic Lesson 9

Lacking the energy of the 9 translates into a lack of tolerance and empathy. You may struggle to identify with the plights of those around you. You must learn to broaden your view, to "walk a mile in their shoes." The karmic lesson of 9 challenges you to give back and to commit time and energy to the wellbeing of others.

KARMIC DEBT NUMBERS

You reap what you sow, and karmic debt numbers represent the consequences in this life of your actions in past lives. These numbers show us the trials and tribulations that we will see repeated over and over again in our lives. The power of karmic numbers lies in our ability to learn the lessons they have to teach, thus overcoming them and breaking the cycle, bringing a deep sense of spiritual peace to our lives.

But we cannot overcome patterns we do not recognize, and that's why it's beneficial to know about any karmic debt numbers we may have in our numerological chart. It's vital to remember, though, that these karmic debt numbers do not reflect on anything you've done here in this life. You cannot blame yourself for these circumstances, but you must face them nonetheless. Do not fear them; many people have karmic debts, including myself. Instead, embrace the challenge – the only way out is through.

Do You Have Any Karmic Debt Numbers?

Karmic debt numbers work a little differently from the other numbers we've learned so far. They are not calculated through addition. Instead, you may find the karmic debt numbers 13, 14, 16, or 19 *within* the calculations for your core numbers – as sums before you reduced them to 4, 5, 7, or 1.

To find out whether you have any karmic debt numbers, go back and review your previous calculations. Look at the sums in your name and birthday before you reduced them to single digits. Do you see 13, 14, 16, or 19? If so, you've found a karmic debt number. (It is possible to have several.)

For example, in Chapter One, we practiced with this date of birth:

December 14, 1979
December = 12 = 1 + 2 = 3
14 = 1 + 4 = 5
1979 = 1 + 9 + 7 + 9 = 26 = 2 + 6 = 8
3 + 5 + 8 = 16 = 1 + 6 = 7

So a person born on December 14, 1979, has a life path number of 7 and a karmic debt of 16.

Karmic debt numbers are most influential when you find them in your life path number calculation, but they can be found when calculating any of your core numbers. Outside of your core numbers, 13, 14, 16, and 19 do not indicate karmic debts.

Another example:

Delphina Marie Woods =
D L P H N = 4 + 2 + 7 + 8 + 5 = 26 = 2 + 6 = 8
M R = 4 + 9 = 13 = 1 + 3 = 4

$$W D S = 5 + 4 + 1 = 10 = 1 + 0 = 1$$
$$8 + 4 + 1 = \underline{13} = 1 + 3 = 4$$

In calculating my personality number, the consonants in my name sum to 13 before being reduced to 4, giving me a karmic debt of 13. Because this is in my personality rather than my life path, its influence is reduced.

Now, try it yourself. Go back through your core number calculations and look for a 13, 14, 16, or 19. If you find one or more, record them in your chart in your notebook, and keep reading to learn how you can free yourself of your karmic burdens and leave the cycle once and for all!

The Cycles You Must End: The Burdens of Your Karmic Debt Numbers

Karmic Debt 13

The 13 indicates abuse of morality in a past life, often dealing with material gain. As such, with a karmic debt of 13 in your core number calculations, you'll have to work much harder than other people to achieve success in your career. You're likely to run into many roadblocks on the way to acquiring prosperity and stability. You must avoid shortcuts and instead put in a methodical, diligent effort to overcome this karmic influence and make the most of your vocation in this life.

Karmic Debt 14

The 14 springs from abuse of freedom in past lifetimes. With a karmic debt of 14, you must find the balance between free-spiritedness and limitations. Work to put up personal boundaries and keep yourself focused on your goal to avoid going off the rails. This karmic debt is related to escapism, and you'll be challenged many times in your life with tests of your self-control. Maintain moderation to free yourself of this burden, lest you keep on running in this life and the next.

Karmic Debt 16

Karmic debt 16 relates to an abuse of love in a past life and manifests as repeated cycles of heartbreak in this life. Who's heart? Yours or your partner's – it can go either way or even both ways. You must address the toxic patterns in your relationships and cultivate loyalty and honesty in love to free yourself of this karmic burden. Take responsibility for your own actions while simultaneously avoiding partners who do not deserve you.

Karmic Debt 19

Finding a 19 when calculating your core numbers indicates that you abused power in a past life. You're likely to experience many personal problems in this life that you will face alone. Your challenge is to learn to let go and accept the help of others, and to help others in return. Essentially, with this karmic debt number, your goal in this life is to make up for the harm you did to others in the past. Watch your ego, and let go of your control issues.

5

NUMEROLOGICAL CYCLES – THE ELEGANT ARCS OF YOUR PERSONAL STORY

Nature itself is a cycle, constantly moving through seasons, the rotation of the planets, and death and rebirth. By observing the cycles we see in nature, we can glean information about what is likely to come; we know that spring blooms will surely follow winter frosts.

So, too, this universal law plays out in numerology. Numbers repeat in a continuous cycle, and as the numbers on the calendar progress through their seasonal changes, these unique vibrations ebb and flow from our lives – and by recognizing the pattern, we can predict what is to come.

Numbers cycle through our lives in different ways and at different intervals. There are nine-year-long cycles, annual cycles, even daily cycles – and each one has a specific effect on the way we think, feel, and behave as we experience the cycling vibrations of these numbers.

There are both personal and universal cycles in numerology. Universal cycles are based on calendar dates; they occur on a broad scale and tell us about universal trends. In contrast, personal cycles are based on your date of birth, and their influence is unique to you.

Some personal cycles have a prolonged effect and influence us over the entire course of our lives. These are the period cycles (also called life cycles), pinnacle cycles, and challenges (or life challenges, which we'll cover in Chapter Six). The remaining personal cycles are the personal day cycle, personal month cycle, and personal year cycle. These are like your own spiritual calendar, with each period in time represented by the energies of single-digit numbers 1-9 in a continuous loop.

We'll begin with the period cycles, which give us the overarching structure of the story of your life.

PERIOD CYCLES

Just as there are three acts in most traditional plays, the stories of our lives follow a "three-act" structure, if we live long enough to see them to their natural end.

Just like your life path number, your period cycles are based on your date of birth, and like your other personal cycles, are closely related to your life path. The exact period of your life when each cycle begins and ends is variable, and based on your life path number. Use the chart below to determine when your first, second, and third-period cycles begin and end, and note this in your chart.

Your Life Path	1st Period Cycle	2nd Period Cycle	3rd Period Cycle
Life Path 1	Birth to Age 26/35*	Age 26/35 to 53/62*	Age 53/63+*
Life Path 2	Birth to Age 34	Age 34 to Age 61	Age 61+
Life Path 3	Birth to Age 33	Age 33 to Age 60	Age 60+
Life Path 4	Birth to Age 32	Age 32 to Age 59	Age 59+
Life Path 5	Birth to Age 31	Age 31 to Age 58	Age 58+
Life Path 6	Birth to Age 30	Age 30 to Age 57	Age 57+
Life Path 7	Birth to Age 29	Age 29 to Age 56	Age 56+
Life Path 8	Birth to Age 28	Age 28 to Age 55	Age 55+
Life Path 9	Birth to Age 27	Age 27 to Age 54	Age 54+
Life Path 11	Birth to Age 26/34*	Age 26/34 to 53/61*	Age 53/61+*
Life Path 22	Birth to Age 15/33*	Age 15/33 to 42/60*	Age 42/60+*

*I have included two ages of division for life path 1 because there is some disagreement among numerologists on these dates. Some contend that those with a life path of 1 start right out of the gate as the pioneers they're meant to be. Because they begin their lives on a personal year cycle, some numerologists believe that life path 1s have concluded their first period by the time they are only 26.

In my experience, not everyone who dives in headfirst, as the 1 is prone to do, will mature so early. Sometimes, these individuals take a wrong turn at a young age and need another 9-year go-around to get it right. See for yourself which one fits your life story best.

Some numerologists believe that a life path of master numbers 11 or 22 can be read two ways, depending on whether the person is an old soul or a young soul. If you feel there was a great turning point in your life at age 26 or 15, respectively, use those numbers, but if you feel your turning point was closer to age 33/34, use those.

First Period Cycle

The first period cycle is with you from the beginning of your life and lasts about thirty years. See the chart above to determine the precise year based on your life path number. The influence of this number is mostly felt from your teen years on, since in childhood we are heavily influenced by vibrations outside of ourselves; infants are, after all, dependent on adults.

During your first period cycle, you are groping around for your true nature but have not yet fully grasped yourself. As you are coming into your own, you're dealing with powerful forces that surround you. In story arc terms, the first period is the inciting incident in your life, because it is here where you begin your story.

The transition between your first and second period cycles can be quite jarring, since it's the first such transition you experience in life.

Your first period cycle is based on your month of birth. Use the table below to find the number that corresponds to your first period cycle. Record this number in your chart, and read on to find out what it means for your formative years.

January	February	March	April	May	June
1	2	3	4	5	6
July	August	September	October	November	December
7	8	9	10	11	12

First Period 1 (Born in January or October):

Your first period cycle is a time of great progress and intensity. You will be called upon to exercise every one of your talents to persevere. Life's hard knocks will test your resiliency, but you'll emerge much stronger. You'll need to be brave, strong, and independent, and these qualities will shape your personality as you mature.

First Period 2 (Born in February):

Your first 30 or so years are a period of gradual development. Your progress is slow but steady. During this time, your partnerships are particularly important to you, and you will cultivate tact and diplomacy. Your personality will be shaped by your intuitive gifts, and artistic talents may first show themselves in this period of your life.

First Period 3 (Born in March or December):

Your early years are a period of heightened self-expression and great social activity; you'll make many friends. You'll realize a creative talent at an early age. Your dedication will be tested, however, and you'll need to learn the virtues of focus and self-discipline to bring your talents to new heights.

First Period 4 (Born in April)

The first period of your life will be full of hard work, as well as the rewards it brings. During this time, you're principally concerned with building a solid foundation for your life through career, family, and community. You'll need discipline, motivation, and analytical skills to make the most of this time.

First Period 5 (Born in May)

Your first 30 or so years are a time of rapid change. You'll learn many lessons and cultivate an appreciation for freedom. You'll likely travel or change residency many times during this period, and as such, you'll meet many people, helping you build tolerance and communication skills. To succeed during these years, you'll need to grab life by the horns.

First Period 6 (Born in June)

Your first period cycle is a time of responsibility to your family. The value of commitment will come into sharp focus for you during these years, and it will be a time of harmony in your relationships. The people around you need you, love you, and appreciate you. This is a good time for marriage or starting a business partnership, during which you'll cultivate a flexible, cooperative nature.

First Period 7 (Born in July)

You'll spend the first three decades of your life as a student, either literally or figuratively, studying something you love in-depth and learning all there is to know about it. By the end of this period, you'll be an expert at it. Not too focused on relationships, you'll spend this time sharpening your mind. You'll need to practice focus and self-reflection to make the most of your abilities.

First Period 8 (Born in August)

With 8 for your first period cycle, this time is perfect for your career and presents opportunities for great financial reward. The trick will be having resilience after setbacks and difficulties. You will be challenged to learn new ways to approach problems, and your leadership skills will be tested. You'll have access to significant power during this period in life, but it's up to you to harness it for your own good.

First Period 9 (Born in September)

The first 30 years or so of your life are spent dedicated to the well-being of others. You'll develop compassion and tolerance and come to understand unconditional love. You won't reach the pinnacle of your humanitarian ideals in this period, but you will strive toward them valiantly and achieve much personal growth. You'll be challenged to live up to your own high moral standards.

First Period 11 (Born in November)

Your first period cycle is a time of idealism and spiritual illumination. You will end this cycle more spiritually evolved than others of your age, provided you focus your efforts. This is not a time to work towards personal gains; you must embrace the path that leads to your high ideals.

Second Period Cycle

This cycle is the second act of our lives, when the action slowly rises and the tension builds. With it, we welcome gradual growth, and the slow emergence of our talents and wisdom, as if watching flowers bloom. The first part of this cycle is about our challenge to find our place in this world, while in our late 30s and onward we begin to realize self-mastery.

Your second period begins when your first one ends, and lasts 27 years, until its influence fades to welcome in the third-period cycle.

Like your birthday number, your second period cycle is calculated based on the day of the month on which you were born. This time, however, you'll reduce the number. For example, if you were born on the 31st, your second period cycle is 4, because 3 + 1 = 4. The only exceptions here are the master numbers 11 and 22. Don't reduce these for your second period cycle.

Now, find your second period cycle number, record it in your chart, and let's find out what the middle period of your life has in store.

Second Period 1 (Born on the 1st, 10th, 19th, or 28th)

Your second period cycle is defined by self-empower-ment. You will experience intense personal growth during this time, facilitated by difficult life circum-stances that you must summon the courage to navigate. You'll be called upon to exercise strength and leader-ship skills, and you'll come out of all this with a solid sense of self-confidence.

Second Period 2 (Born on the 2nd or 20th)

With 2 ruling the middle of your life, this is a time for you to dig deep and develop your sensitivity and intu-itive powers. During these years, you are drawn to others and will cultivate many deep, personal relation-ships, but you may become emotionally fragile. Your challenge will be to keep your head straight and your feet on the ground during all this development of the heart. If you have artistic talent, this is a good period to spend devoted to your art.

Second Period 3 (Born on the 3rd, 12th, 21st, or 30th)

While the second period cycle is typically marked by maturity, you may feel during this time that your mind is growing especially spry and youthful. This is an excellent period in your life for creative endeavors, but you'll need to cultivate discipline and focus to reach your goals. You have quite a lot of charisma and charm, and you'll likely enjoy a broad, supportive social circle during these middle years of your life.

Second Period 4 (Born on the 4th, 13th, or 31st)

The middle period of your life is a time for hard work and diligence, and you'll reap the benefits of both personal success and a deep feeling of accomplishment. You are driven by the need to support your family and community. This is not a time for lofty dreams; instead, your organizational skills and motivation will be tested before you gain material rewards.

Second Period 5 (Born on the 5th, 14th, or 23rd)

Your second period cycle is a time of dynamic change. While others may be settling into routines in their middle years, you're on the move. Avoid predictability; it will not serve you. You'll meet many interesting people during this time and encounter many new ideas. This will require you to be highly adaptable, but in exchange, you'll develop a marvelously open-minded perspective on life.

Second Period 6 (Born on the 6th, 15th, or 24th)

The middle years of your life are marked by a sense of duty and responsibility. The people in your life depend on you for emotional support. You will be called upon to nurture your familial and community relationships, but to succeed, you must be willing to compromise. This is an excellent period in your life for marriage or for starting a business venture.

Second Period 7 (Born on the 7th, 16th, or 25th)

This is a time of intellectual exploration for you. You will feel called to delve into some of the deepest mysteries and biggest questions in life. During these years, you'll experience significant intellectual and spiritual growth, but this is not a time to focus on relationships. You may resist sharing your thoughts and feelings with others, but you must push through this. You're a teacher at heart.

Second Period 8 (Born on the 8th, 16th, or 26th)

During the middle years of your life, you will have immense power at your fingertips. This time is ripe for financial and career success, but you must use your skills purposefully and smartly to succeed. Don't cut corners; avoid "get rich quick" schemes. On the other hand, be willing to take risks in order to reap rewards.

Second Period 9 (Born on the 9th, 18th, or 27th)

The middle years of your life are a time to pursue humanitarian efforts and devote yourself to the betterment of your community. Your effort and hard work will be rewarded, but only if you remain focused on the pursuit of your high ideals. Do not fall back into self-service. You will be asked to let go, to sacrifice something of yourself, but in return, you'll experience amazing spiritual gains.

Second Period 11 (Born on the 11th or 29th)

With master number 11 ruling your second period cycle, this is a time of spiritual advancement for you, during which you will accumulate much wisdom. You seek higher ideals, but you're at risk of having your head too far in the clouds to see any tangible benefit from this growth. Work on bettering yourself so you can better serve your world.

Second Period 22 (Born on the 22nd)

With master number 22 ruling your second period cycle, you have the capacity to create something wonderful during these years, to manifest your dreams. Your talents are at their peak during this time, and you feel called to teach all that you have learned, to pass it on to others. You must commit yourself entirely to this work, lest you waste your potential.

Third Period Cycle

The third and final life cycle represents the climax and denouement of our lives. It lasts from the end of the second period until death.

This last period cycle is like harvest time for our souls; the flowers that bloomed in the second period have produced ripe fruit. During this cycle, your self-expression is at a high, as is your personal power.

To calculate your third period cycle, sum the four digits of your year of birth. Stop reducing when you reach either a single digit or a master number. For example:

$$2001 = 2 + 0 + 0 + 1 = 3$$
$$1984 = 1 + 9 + 8 + 4 = 22$$
$$1949 = 1 + 9 + 4 + 9 = 23 = 2 + 3 = 5$$

Calculate the number of your second period cycle and record your result in your numerological chart so we can discover what the final years of your life have in store.

Third Period 1

Your third-period cycle will see you in a leadership role, and you may find yourself moving towards a new goal in life. While others around you seem to be slowing down in their later years, you will experience a renewed inner drive and feel young at heart. You'll need much perseverance to reach your goals – take care not to let your detractors get to you.

Third Period 2

In your later years, you'll find yourself developing a deeper, more intuitive connection to the world around you. You'll rely on your heart over your head and learn to trust your instincts. You may find that you don't hold back your thoughts and feelings like you used to. Others are drawn to you. You may discover a new talent late in your life.

Third Period 3

With 3 ruling your third life period, you may feel as though you've drunk from the fountain of youth! Bursting with energy and creative ideas, your magnetic personality draws people to you. You run the risk, however, of wasting your ideas and talents if you do not cultivate focus. You may have trouble discerning which of your ideas are brilliant and which should be discarded.

Third Period 4

You'll stay busy during the final years of your life. Not one for retirement, you'll either continue working or devote yourself to a new hobby or volunteer project. Your home and finances remain important to you, as you've worked hard all your life to build the foundation on which your final years rest. Your family is a large part of this period for you.

Third Period 5

You may find yourself drawn to travel in your later years. Others may find your free-spirited lifestyle inappropriate for your age, but the 5 encourages you to be spontaneous, so you'll reap rewards others might miss. Stay social and use this opportunity to open your mind to new perspectives and ways of being. Don't put too much faith in your plans, as they are liable to change quickly.

Third Period 6

During the last years of your life, family will be your primary focus. Rather than being cared for by others, like many your age, you will still be the caregiver in the family, which will bring you great satisfaction. This cycle is perfect for a family-run business and for grandchildren. You will discover increased opportunities during this period to express your creative self.

Third Period 7

Your third-period cycle is defined by wisdom, and the final years of your life will be full of revelation and personal discovery. This is a time to turn inward and explore your spiritual and intellectual sides. This will bring you peace and harmony inside, but your interpersonal relationships may suffer. You are prone to self-isolation during these years.

Third Period 8

Your third-period cycle is a time of personal power and authority. Retirement is unlikely, as your leadership skills are at their peak, and you see opportunity all around you. You are likely to accumulate financial wealth, but there is a risk of financial loss. Riding the rollercoaster of success will teach you a valuable lesson of detachment.

Third Period 9

The final period of your life finds you striving to give back; you will do well in volunteer work. Your humanitarian ideals shine through, and your open-minded attitude and wisdom will guide you toward success in selfless endeavors. You have a strong sense of justice and may find yourself drawn to politics. Your creativity will also increase during this time.

Third Period 11

With master number 11 ruling the final years of your life, you'll find yourself increasingly relying on your intuition. You'll grow spiritually and shed layers of inhibition to embrace your true self. You will find your voice, and others will be drawn to you, especially young people. You are likely to discover a new talent during these years that was previously unknown to you.

Third Period 22

With master number 22 ruling your third-period cycle, you have an immense potential to lead and teach others. Not only have you gained valuable wisdom during your life that you're ready to share, but you have the practical mind and the energy to make your ideas tangible. You'll stay very busy in your retirement with humanitarian projects.

PINNACLE CYCLES

Each of us has four pinnacle cycles in our lives, which represent the major lessons we are to learn on our life path. These are the most important of the personal cycles in numerology. While the period cycles tell us about our personal growth, the pinnacle cycles reveal the external influences that we must face.

Your first pinnacle cycle, like your first period cycle, lasts until about 30. The second and third pinnacle cycles last 9 years each, and the fourth remains with you for the rest of your life.

The actual ages of transition between one pinnacle cycle and the next are crucial. These are often ages of great change and potential. Numerologists call these "turning points," and they last for about a two-year period around each pinnacle's beginning and end.

Like your period cycles, the delineating dates of your pinnacle cycles are determined by your life path number. Use the table below to determine when your first, second, third, and fourth pinnacle cycles begin and end and note this in the chart you've created in your notebook.

Life Path	1st Pinnacle	2nd Pinnacle	3rd Pinnacle	4th Pinnacle
Life Path 1	Birth to Age 35	Age 35-44	Age 44-53	Age 53+
Life Path 2	Birth to Age 34	Age 34-43	Age 43-52	Age 52+
Life Path 3	Birth to Age 33	Age 33-42	Age 42-51	Age 51+
Life Path 4	Birth to Age 32	Age 32-41	Age 41-50	Age 50+
Life Path 5	Birth to Age 31	Age 31-40	Age 40-49	Age 49+
Life Path 6	Birth to Age 30	Age 30-39	Age 39-48	Age 48+
Life Path 7	Birth to Age 29	Age 29-38	Age 38-47	Age 47+
Life Path 8	Birth to Age 28	Age 28-37	Age 37-46	Age 46+
Life Path 9	Birth to Age 27	Age 27-36	Age 36-45	Age 45+
Life Path 11	Birth to Age 34	Age 34-43	Age 43-52	Age 52+
Life Path 22	Birth to Age 32	Age 32-41	Age 41-50	Age 50+

First Pinnacle Cycle

To calculate your first pinnacle cycle, you will reduce your month of birth and your day of birth separately using addition. Then, you'll add these two numbers together and reduce again to find a single-digit or master number.

For example:

October 28
October = 10 = 1 + 0 = 1
28 = 2 + 8 = 10 = 1 + 0 = 1
1 + 1 = 2

So a person born on the 28th of October has a first pinnacle cycle of 2.

Remember, leave your birth year out of this equation and stop reducing if you reach a master number. Record the number of your first pinnacle cycle in your numerological chart.

First Pinnacle 1

Your first pinnacle cycle will find you relying on yourself without much support from those around you. You'll develop independence, resiliency, and initiative. Your lesson will be to bounce back after difficult setbacks. Don't give in to self-pity, but instead cultivate strength of will.

First Pinnacle 2

Your first pinnacle cycle will help you to grow up sensitive and intuitive. You will require patience to develop your insight and instinct. Your lesson is to use diplomacy and subtle persuasion to achieve your goals, because direct approaches won't serve you well. Use your gifts to bring peace to your relationships.

First Pinnacle 3

Your first pinnacle cycle is a very creative time for you, during which your self-expression and artistic talents are greatly enhanced. Your lesson will be to apply yourself. With a focused discipline in the arts, you'll experience much success. You'll have a broad social circle during these years and develop strong emotional connections with many people in your life.

First Pinnacle 4

Your first pinnacle cycle will be full of hard work, but this will be an opportunity to reap many rewards. You're dependable, reliable, and great at what you do, but your lesson will be to learn to cooperate with others. You are so focused on your work that you have a tendency to seem dismissive to others, but you won't meet your life goals without their help.

First Pinnacle 5

You will learn many lessons during your first pinnacle cycle, and life experience is your best teacher. This is a time for experimentation, not for settling down. You'll travel and meet people from all walks of life, having many adventures and learning about the world. Your talents for writing and speaking will serve you well.

First Pinnacle 6

The first pinnacle cycle for you will be all about your family and community. You'll take on many responsibilities and duties during this time. Do not think of this as a burden; if you rise to the occasion, you'll gain valuable experience and new perspectives. You'll learn to manage your emotions during these years and will have much compassion and tenderness to offer others.

First Pinnacle 7

The first pinnacle of 7 suggests an early period of soul searching. You'll spend a lot of time alone developing a rich inner life, concerned with grand and spiritual matters. You're likely to develop a great sense of faith during these years. Your lesson is to not lose sight of the people in your life as you delve deeply into yourself.

First Pinnacle 8

With an 8 for your first pinnacle cycle, the early years of your life will be a time of material growth and financial gain. Your good judgment and visionary attitude mean that you'll have a talent for business and finance. Your lesson is to share your wealth with others in order to continue the cycle of prosperity. If you do not, you risk spiritual demise.

First Pinnacle 9

In your first pinnacle cycle, you'll be involved in a project bigger than yourself – perhaps social activism. You will find satisfaction in providing for others. You'll make a great business owner in these early years, as knowing you provide a living for your workers will make you feel whole. Your lesson will be to learn to take care of yourself before others.

First Pinnacle 11

Your first pinnacle cycle will bring many challenges with master number 11. This is a high point of sensitivity and intuition, and with so much going on spiritually and psychologically, you are at risk of losing yourself to anxieties. You must keep your feet on the ground and keep faith in your heart.

First Pinnacle 22

Under master number 22, your first pinnacle cycle will ask a lot of you. This is a demanding time in your life, when you will be tested regularly. You'll be tempted to give in to the pressure, but if you push through, there will be great rewards. Your power is immense and you have the ability to create something spectacular during these years.

Second Pinnacle Cycle

To calculate your second pinnacle cycle, reduce your day of birth and your year of birth separately. Then, add these two numbers together and reduce again to find a single-digit or master number. For example:

$$31, 1987$$
$$31 = 3 + 1 = 4$$
$$1987 = 1 + 9 + 8 + 7 = 25 = 2 + 5 = 7$$
$$4 + 7 = 11$$

So someone born on the 31st of the month in the year 1987 has a second pinnacle cycle of 11.

Calculate your second pinnacle cycle number and record it in your numerological chart. Be sure to leave your birth month out of this equation and stop reducing when you reach a master number.

Second Pinnacle 1

Your second pinnacle cycle will be a time of rapid growth and significant self-improvement. Life will throw many curve balls your way, and you'll need to call upon every gift you are given to overcome them. Your lesson is not to become self-centered or dismiss others' ideas. You must be flexible and open to the counsel of others in order to succeed.

Second Pinnacle 2

Your second pinnacle cycle will find you in the role of mediator. You will be the glue that keeps others together. However, you are very sensitive to criticism. Don't indulge these feelings. Your challenge will be to find and preserve balance in all things. You will work harmoniously with others during these years.

Second Pinnacle 3

Your second pinnacle cycle will be a highly emotional time for you, with many social experiences. You will attract many friends and loved ones and have the ability to inspire and motivate others with your optimism. This is a lucky time in your life, when you will be able to overcome problems with less effort than others, as long as you stay in touch with your emotions.

Second Pinnacle 4

Your second pinnacle cycle is a time of great industrialism – you'll complete many goals and make considerable progress towards your dreams. You may also find yourself caring for others' physical needs; family is an important part of your life during this time. Your lesson will be to not get bogged down in the details or frustrated when things don't go your way.

Second Pinnacle 5

You will find yourself in a state of flux during your second pinnacle cycle. Your challenge will be to find your footing; stick with a particular discipline or nurture one relationship. You must learn that having a home base won't limit your freedom but will instead give you a safe place to return home to – literally and emotionally. You have an addictive personality and should be vigilant about substance abuse during this time.

Second Pinnacle 6

Your second pinnacle cycle is defined by love and warmth. This is an excellent time in your life to get married or have children, as it is a time for your family to grow. You have much love to give! Your challenge will be to grow and learn in your relationships. You will need to settle conflicts with compromise.

Second Pinnacle 7

Your second pinnacle cycle is a time of inward development. You will find yourself drawn to contemplating your truest nature, and your intuition will sharpen, which will reveal to you the path ahead. Your challenge

is to not shy away from the wisdom you seek to gain –
nor to avoid the difficult truths you will need to accept
about yourself and the world around you.

Second Pinnacle 8

Your second pinnacle cycle will see you with many
achievements and great prosperity. You will appear to
have the Midas touch, and with your confidence, wit,
and ambition, you have everything you need to realize
all your dreams. Your challenge will be not letting your
power go to your head; you must be a gentle leader, not
a tyrannical dictator, in both your business and
personal life.

Second Pinnacle 9

Your second pinnacle cycle is a great time for spiritual
and financial progress. Your challenge will be to
surrender yourself to your truest calling. You are likely
to discover a new artistic talent during these years,
which may call you to leave an existing business. Take a
risk; you'll only find fulfillment when you live your
truest life.

Second Pinnacle 11

Your second pinnacle cycle, ruled by master number
11, is a time of great adversity and emotional turmoil.
You will have all your values and even your sense of

identity called into question. You may shrink away from the world and seek to find a comfortable, predictable place in life. You will sense that you're being driven towards a greater destiny, and you must learn to let go and surrender to the universe.

Second Pinnacle 22

With master number 22 ruling your second pinnacle cycle, you have an enormous responsibility on your shoulders during these years. You'll find both your mental and physical skills at their maximum, but you will also be susceptible to all the internal pressures this brings. You must find the determination to push through obstacles. If you do, you will leave a lasting impact on the world.

Third Pinnacle Cycle

The third pinnacle covers approximately the decade of our 40s. This cycle tends to be the most productive time in our lives.

To get your third pinnacle cycle number, simply add your first and second period cycle numbers together and reduce as needed to reach a single digit or a master number. Perform this quick calculation and record your third pinnacle cycle in your chart.

Third Pinnacle 1

Your third pinnacle cycle will test all your faculties, but it promises incredible rewards. You will need both an iron will and adaptability to pull through this time in your life, and in exchange, you will discover the stuff you are made of. Many hidden talents will reveal themselves to you during this time. You must have faith in yourself that you will make it through adversity.

Third Pinnacle 2

Your third pinnacle cycle will be a time of great emotional development and sensitivity. You'll seek out harmony and beauty, but what you really need is to face difficult truths. Your challenge will be to grow your self-confidence and learn to use your voice while keeping an open heart towards the world. Do not give in to your fears, or you are likely to languish in emotional turmoil.

Third Pinnacle 3

During the third pinnacle cycle in your life, you will lack discipline and focus. Diligent effort will be the key to productivity. You will be especially susceptible to impulsivity and should take extra care with your financial and relationship decisions during this time. Your challenge will be to learn your limits.

Third Pinnacle 4

Your third pinnacle cycle will be an especially productive time in your life, and you're even likely to be a bit of a workaholic during these years. You are the foundation of your business life and personal life, and people depend on you. This responsibility can be daunting, and your perfectionism will lead you to self-doubt and undue self-criticism. Your challenge will be to not become bogged down in the details.

Third Pinnacle 5

Your third pinnacle cycle will teach you the value of letting go. You will be called to pursue your freedom during this period, which will cause strife in your relationships and work life. But through this, you will learn how to love unconditionally; that to hold on tightly to a person, place, or job is to place conditions on your love for that thing. Your challenge will be to not shy away from this – maintaining superficial relationships to maintain the status quo will hold back both you and your loved ones.

Third Pinnacle 6

Your third pinnacle cycle will be marked by harmonious relationships and business matters. This is the perfect time to start a business or grow your financial portfolio. You'll attract many people to you and would do well in the role of teacher or healer. Your talents will truly shine during these years. Your challenge will be to maintain balance.

Third Pinnacle 7

Your third pinnacle cycle is a time of great spiritual growth and intellectual blossoming. You've cultivated wisdom in your life and have laid the path to contentment in your old age. Your challenge will be to avoid cynicism. You may find that you don't relate to other people or consider yourself to be one of them, but life is bound to remind you that you are human, too.

Third Pinnacle 8

Your third pinnacle cycle will present you with opportunities beyond your wildest dreams. Your challenge will be to hold fast to your values in the face of the temptation to place financial gains above all else. You are very susceptible to greed and must practice both altruism and balance. You are being tested – you must learn the real value of money, lest you face spiritual downfall.

Third Pinnacle 9

Your third pinnacle cycle will be a time of social responsibility. You will feel deep compassion for humanitarian causes and be called to help the less fortunate. Your challenge will be to nurture yourself and your personal relationships when guilt and negative self-talk push you to devote so much of yourself to the greater good.

Third Pinnacle 11

Ruled by master number 11, your third pinnacle cycle will find you in a heightened spiritual state. You'll discover you can see things more clearly than ever before, which is both a blessing and a curse. You may feel out of touch with the rest of the world because you are aware of so much more than those around you. Your challenge will be to remain grounded and active in your community and relationships.

Third Pinnacle 22

With master number 22 for your third pinnacle cycle, this will be a very challenging and demanding time in your life. You have everything within you that you need to succeed, but you will be tested to your limits and endure many struggles. Your challenge will be to lean on your friends, family, and supporters to help you, because without those relationships to bolster your self-confidence, the challenges you'll face may break you.

Fourth Pinnacle Cycle

Your fourth pinnacle cycle covers the last period of your life, from about age 50 onward. To calculate your fourth pinnacle cycle, reduce your month of birth and your year of birth separately. Then add these two numbers together and reduce them to find a single-digit or master number. For example:

$$September\ 2000$$
$$September = 9$$
$$2000 = 2 + 0 + 0 + 0 = 2$$
$$9 + 2 = 11$$

Therefore, someone born in September of 2000 has a second pinnacle cycle of 11.

Calculate your fourth pinnacle cycle number now and record the result in your numerological chart. Remember to leave the day of the month you were born out of this equation and stop reducing if you reach a master number.

Fourth Pinnacle 1

During your fourth pinnacle cycle, you must keep your dreams in sight. Don't lose confidence, and stay focused on your vision. You'll have many innovative ideas and the necessary skills at this point in your life to turn them into reality. During these years, you'll make an excellent leader or politician, and you'll have many opportunities for success.

Fourth Pinnacle 2

Your fourth pinnacle cycle is a highly sensitive time in your life. You'll surround yourself with beauty and seek out harmonious environments. You may have an inclination to take up a new artistic talent, particularly playing an instrument. The people in your life love and appreciate you, so remember your worth and don't stew about acknowledgments that aren't verbalized.

Fourth Pinnacle 3

Your fourth pinnacle cycle is an especially creative and artistic period in your life. Make the most of these abilities by applying your talents with discipline. You'll have a heightened chance of success and prosperity during these years, but only if you pursue your art fearlessly.

Fourth Pinnacle 4

Your fourth pinnacle cycle will be defined by hard work and the rewards that come along with it. You would do well to remind yourself that the best things take time, and even slow progress is still progress. Don't rush yourself; use your skills to be methodical and efficient in your work. All work and no play will drain you quickly, so make sure you let go and live a little during this time.

Fourth Pinnacle 5

Your challenge during this period is to accept your limitations. You crave freedom and hate to feel tied down, but you must understand that without limitations, there would be no sense of freedom to enjoy. This time in your life is ideal for your communication talents, and you'd make a great salesperson.

Fourth Pinnacle 6

Your last pinnacle cycle is marked by emotional growth and progress. With your drive to help others, you will spend this time developing into a compassionate partner or parent, a level-headed business person, or even a pillar of your community. You must guard against spreading yourself too thin, however, and remember to take care of yourself.

Fourth Pinnacle 7

During your last pinnacle cycle, you'll find great insight and work to refine yourself as a person. Remember that perfection is not a realistic ambition. With a hyper-critical attitude, you'll never be satisfied, and your relationships will suffer. Take care to grow in the right direction spiritually during this time, and you'll reap the rewards of true contentment.

Fourth Pinnacle 8

Your fourth pinnacle cycle is a time of prosperity, both financially and spiritually – provided you keep your ideals high. This period will afford you many opportunities for growth and bless you with the gift of balance, especially when it comes to financial decisions. This is an excellent time for investments.

Fourth Pinnacle 9

Your final pinnacle cycle is defined by success, and maybe even fame! You may feel drawn to spirituality or philosophical pursuits, and you would make an excellent teacher or healer. You'll have opportunities to travel and meet many different people, which will only help your compassionate nature to grow.

Fourth Pinnacle 11

During the fourth pinnacle cycle of your life, ruled by master number 11, you will be at your most creative and inventive. Follow your intuition; it will lead you to incredible things, including great peace. You'll receive many rewards on the physical, mental, and spiritual planes during this time.

Fourth Pinnacle 22

Ruled by master number 22, your fourth pinnacle cycle is all about big things: big dreams, big plans, and big accomplishments. You must devote yourself unwaveringly to your dream in order to achieve it, however. Without ambition, you'll languish in boredom during your later years and your talents will waste away.

MATURITY NUMBER

Our maturity number in numerology indicates our level of emotional and spiritual maturation, as its name implies. Sometimes called the reality number or realization number, our maturity number can tell us a lot about our mission in life. It relates to the lessons we learn during our earlier years, so you may find yourself giving less and less thought to the things that once held you back, until one day they're not on your radar at all.

This number's influence doesn't "kick in" until later in life. The period and pinnacle cycles we just calculated have specific, measurable start and end dates based on your life path, but with the maturity number, the onset is a little hazy. Its influence will come on gradually, sometime between age 30-35, and build throughout your 30s and into your 40s, and even 50s. Once it reaches its peak, it will continue to affect the remainder of your life.

Calculating Your Maturity Number

Your maturity number is calculated on both your date of birth and your name. To find your maturity number, simply sum your life path and expression numbers together and reduce as necessary. Since this is neither one of the major cycles nor a core number in your chart, you can reduce master numbers wherever they appear.

For instance, if your life path number is 11 and your expression is nine, your maturity number is 2:

$$11 + 9 = 20 = 2 + 0 = 2$$

Perform this quick calculation and record your maturity number in your chart, then read on to discover your personal glow-up.

Your Next Evolution: What Your Maturity Number Has in Store

Maturity 1

With a maturity of 1, as you age, you'll feel a shift related to independence. You may experience a strong drive to break away from dependencies you held earlier in life. Your financial situation may change drastically, and you will be called to evaluate your self-defeating behaviors.

Maturity 2

With maturity number 2, you'll find yourself reevaluating what it means to serve others. You may find that you've been a doormat, and as you age, you'll start to stand up for yourself more often. You'll also work to understand how you have failed others by being insensitive and learn to appreciate the value of authentic, equal teamwork.

Maturity 3

Under maturity number 3, you're likely to experience a shift related to creativity as you grow older. You'll be called to a life in the arts, drama, music, or perhaps communication, breaking free to do your own thing creatively. This shift will bring you great joy, abundance, and peace.

Maturity 4

With a maturity of 4, you're a hard worker who will come to understand your limitations as you mature. You will learn the value of flexibility and that you can only go so far if you stick to your stubborn and rigid ways. You'll have to examine your sense of responsibility, and you'll come out of it as a better leader and family member, who is less inclined to micromanage.

Maturity 5

Ruled by the 5, your maturity number is all about freedom. You'll likely experience a sudden shift in your life, such as divorce, children leaving home, or the death of a loved one, which will drastically change your sense of freedom and force you to accept the balance of choice and limitation. You may struggle with over-indulgence, such as with substance abuse or overeating, but at the same time, your later years will be filled with exciting travels.

Maturity 6

The 6 is a great number for maturity, and indicates that you may experience a very comfortable financial future. You'll be highly involved in your family life and are likely to have many grandchildren. By this age, you've learned the meaning of unconditional love, and you no longer make room in your life for anything less. You're also likely to find success in a creative endeavor during your later years.

Maturity 7

The maturity number is a fortuitous placement for the 7, which is all about self-reflection and wisdom. You'll reach new spiritual heights and rest easy in your later years, knowing that you've plumbed all the deep questions of life and found satisfactory answers. On the flip side, this change in perspective could come about from a drastic shift in your life, such as divorce, and you're likely to spend time in self-imposed isolation as a result.

Maturity 8

With a maturity number of 8, you will cultivate balance and moderation as you age. Your later years will bring about much achievement and financial gain, but at the same time, you'll come to understand that the true value of money is in sharing it. You may experience a dramatic shift in your career to accommodate your newfound passion for giving back.

Maturity 9

With a maturity number of 9, your final project in life will be a great humanitarian cause. You'll mature into a selfless person and learn to surrender to your spiritual guides. You may be called to a path of teaching, healing, or philanthropy. You're well-equipped to give of yourself in your later years because you've learned how to meet your own needs as well as the needs of others.

6

THE CHALLENGES ON YOUR LIFE'S PATH

There is yet a third long-term personal cycle that bears examination: numerology's challenges. These numbers represent our cycles of strengths and weaknesses throughout our lives and call us to the challenge of embodying the best qualities of these numbers. Numerology also reveals to us the balance number, a gift for overcoming these challenges.

THE CHALLENGES

Like your period and pinnacle cycles, the challenges are derived from your life path and relate closely to your purpose in this life. The challenges will *test* you in order to *teach* you. Don't be discouraged by your challenges;

they are there to help on your life's path, if only you will draw inspiration from them.

The challenges represent a cycle of learning from our weaknesses to develop them into strengths. With each challenge, we are called upon to embody the best qualities of these numbers while shedding their self-destructive and unproductive habits.

There are four principal challenges in numerology. The first is in effect for the early period of your life, from birth to about age 30-35. The second challenge kicks in after that and lasts until about age 55-60. The third challenge is also called the main challenge, and it is with you your whole life. The fourth and final challenge shows up from about age 55-60 on.

Challenges are quite interesting in numerology because they are calculated with *subtraction*. For this reason, the 0 is a possible result for the first time in your numerological chart. Recall that 0 is the nothingness before all existence: pure potential. The 0 is all or nothing. It is up to you to decide your fate.

First Challenge

To calculate your first challenge number, first sum your day of birth and month of birth individually, reducing any master numbers, like so:

April 23

April = 4

23 = 2 + 3 = 5

Now *subtract* the two numbers. It doesn't matter which number you subtract from which, as there are no negative numbers in numerology. You will use the "absolute value" of the number, so it will always be a positive number. Continuing the example from above:

4 - 5 = |-1| = 1 (the absolute value)

A person born on April 23, then, has a first challenge of 1. There is also the possibility of a 0 result. For example:

September 27

September = 9

27 = 2 + 7 = 9

September 27 = 9 - 9 = 0

Let's review one more example to make sure you've got it down. Remember to reduce any master numbers you encounter:

November 5
November = 11 = 1 + 1 = 2
5 = 5
November 5 = 2 - 5 = |-3| = 3

Now, calculate your first challenge in your notebook and record the number in your chart. We'll continue on to calculate all four of your challenge numbers before we dive into the specific attributes each number calls you to demonstrate in life.

Second Challenge

The second challenge on your life path comes into play around age 30-35 and lasts until about age 55-60. To calculate your second challenge number, sum your day of birth and year of birth individually, like so:

23rd, 1982
23 = 2 + 3 = 5
1982 = 1 + 9 + 8 + 2 = 20 = 2 + 0 = 2

Now *subtract* the two numbers. Again, it doesn't matter which number you subtract from which, as there are no negative numbers in numerology:

$$5 - 2 = 3$$
$$2 - 5 = |-3| = 3$$

This means that someone born on the 23rd of a month in 1982 has a second challenge of 3. Again, there is a possibility of a 0 result. For example:

$$1st, 2008$$
$$1st = 1$$
$$2008 = 2 + 0 + 0 + 8 = 10 = 1 + 0 = 1$$
$$1 - 1 = 0$$

Don't forget to reduce any master numbers:

$$22nd, 2009$$
$$22nd = 22 = 2 + 2 = 4$$
$$2009 = 2 + 0 + 0 + 9 = 11 = 1 + 1 = 2$$
$$4 - 2 = 2$$

Calculate your second challenge and record the number in your personal chart.

Third (Main) Challenge

The third challenge is more strongly felt than the other three, and its influence lasts our entire lifetime. It is the primary challenge we are being called to overcome.

To calculate your third, or main challenge, simply subtract your first challenge number from your second and use the absolute value. For example, if your first challenge is 8 and your second challenge is 0, your third (main) challenge is 8:

$$8 - 0 = 8$$

And if you first challenge is 2 and your second challenge is 7, your third (main) challenge is 5:

$$2 - 7 = |-5| = 5$$

Perform this quick subtraction to find your third challenge number and record it in your chart.

Fourth Challenge

The fourth and final challenge comes to you at about age 55-60 and will remain with you for the rest of your life. To calculate your fourth challenge number, sum your day of birth and month of birth individually:

October 17
October = 11 = 1 + 1 = 2
17 = 1 + 7 = 8

Now *subtract* the two numbers, using the "absolute value" of the result, like so:

8 - 2 = 6
2 - 8 = |-6| = 6

So anyone born on October 17, regardless of the year of birth, has a fourth challenge of 6. As with the other challenges, a 0 result is possible – and you will reduce any master numbers you encounter:

April 22
April = 4
22 = 2 + 2 = 4
4 - 4 = 0

Calculate your fourth and final challenge in your notebook and record the result in your chart. Now let's learn what each challenge number means.

Embody the Best: The Meanings of Your Challenges

Challenge 0

In numerology, 0 is not so much considered a number as the proverbial well from which all other numbers spring. Thus, 0 represents pure potential. When it appears in your chart, *you* determine whether the 0 is all or nothing.

The 0 doesn't represent a particular challenge as the other numbers do. Instead, it's likely to represent a time with many smaller obstacles rather than be defined by one major challenge. But this is not a "get out of jail free" card. You can think of a challenge 0 as a call to have faith in yourself and your abilities. It's all about *choice*, and if you don't make the intentional decision to be your best self, you've made the default decision to stagnate.

You can either idle away and let the time pass, or you can take this opportunity to go inward and cultivate some amazing personal growth and expansion. With a challenge of 0, you'll be called to use the positive aspects of *all other numbers:* the 1's independence, the 2's diplomacy, the 3's creativity, the 4's hard work, the 5's curiosity, the 6's love, the 7's wisdom, the 8's power, and the 9's humanitarian vision.

Challenge 1

A challenge of 1 is calling you to stand up for yourself and be self-reliant. You must step up to the plate and take responsibility with your own initiative, as success will not simply fall into your lap. You'll need courage and independence to face a challenge of 1. During this period, you should work to cultivate leadership and people skills so you can be your most effective at work – and learn to leave your ego at the door.

This challenge is likely related to a sense of control. You may feel that you're being dominated by others, either professionally or personally, which can lead you to develop a highly competitive personality. Your challenge is to both stand up for yourself and strive for your goals while avoiding a sense of self-righteousness or developing a control-freak streak.

Challenge 2

A challenge number of 2 calls you to develop empathy, both for yourself and others. The 2's energy is all about partnership and diplomacy, and it is a highly sensitive number. When the 2 appears as one of your challenges, you are being called to harness that sensitivity – to make something good of it rather than let it turn you into a fearful, avoidant person. You'll need to find the balance between giving of yourself to others and giving *to yourself*.

You must work in harmony and cooperation, but your challenge is likely that you're just not feeling these things – at all. You might have a deep-seated fear of criticism or of having your ideas ignored, and you have nagging anxiety that everyone you meet is silently judging you. During this time in your life, you'll have trouble asserting yourself and trusting your decisions. This is a time for slow and deliberate growth. Remind yourself not to take anything too personally.

Challenge 3

With a challenge of number 3, you are being asked to examine your feelings and learn to speak from your heart. This is a time for communication and self-expression. You may feel pulled towards creative endeavors, and you'll need to cultivate communication skills to succeed. The 3 has the potential for an incredible amount of joy. You must harness your creative energies to bring peace, love, and happiness into your life.

Your challenge is to take your ideas and feelings seriously. You're prone to scattering your energies and behaving superficially. Maybe you feel pulled in many directions creatively, which can result in a creative block. You know you need to be "out there" making friends and business deals, but you might feel hopeless and even depressed, and the urge to stick your head in the sand is not easy to push past. Trust in yourself and believe that the world wants to hear what you have to say. Keep up the dream despite your worst critics, especially when that critic is yourself.

Challenge 4

When you come to a challenge of 4 on your life path, you are being called to learn the values of hard work, practicality, and self-discipline. You will need to make a detailed plan of action and use all the resources available to you to make it happen. In particular, you'll need patience and understanding in spades.

A challenge of 4 indicates trouble with work – either you don't feel challenged by your work or it is *too* challenging for you. You may find it hard to focus on this aspect of your life, and you're likely to make excuses about your work life, too. You need to cultivate discipline and learn to work within the parameters given to you.

Challenge 5

The energy of the 5 is intense and highly charged, and a challenge of 5 will put you through a good deal of change. This period in your life is marked by restlessness, so you will feel at your core a building desire for personal freedom. To find the freedom you seek, you need to free *your own mind* from your limiting thoughts and behaviors, but mindfulness will not come easily to you!

You may find yourself feeling impulsive, even unstable. You may even feel like you're going a bit crazy at times! While change is indeed inevitable, you must learn to handle it with control, thought, and purpose. You'll be challenged to commit to something rather than evade responsibility with flightiness. You have to reign in your reckless side in order to succeed through the chaos inherent in this challenge.

Challenge 6

With a 6 for a challenge number, you are being called not only to serve others but to find the balance between committing to others and committing to yourself, and you're likely to find it harder than it sounds. The key here is that you cannot eschew your caring nature; you cannot simply avoid commitments to others to nurture yourself. Otherwise, the nurturing energy of the 6 will warp into greed and conceit.

This challenge may be related to codependency and other unhealthy attachment styles in your relationships. You may find that you hold people in your life to very high standards or that you let them walk all over you. Either habit needs to be addressed during this time in your life. Ultimately, the 6 asks you to embrace unconditional love, to accept both yourself and others.

Challenge 7

With a challenge number of 7, you are called to inner exploration. You'll find yourself contemplating the intricacies of life, the big questions, and see yourself on a path to spiritual growth. You'll be faced with both inner difficulties and external obstacles. Remember that every difficult experience in life, like every bit of knowledge you gain from soul-searching, fuels your betterment. Becoming a master is slow work, and it requires that you trust yourself.

During this time in your life, you're likely to feel pulled to withdraw from others – isolation and a sense of loneliness are common themes. You may feel detached, as if you can't relate to or share with others, or you may find yourself feeling resentful of others and thinking they're beneath you. Both of these attitudes can lead to repressed feelings. The key is to get out of your head and live in the moment.

Challenge 8

With the 8 for a challenge number, you are being called to step up to the plate and make things happen. This is a period of your life for great achievement, but reaching success is, itself, your obstacle. With an 8 challenge, you'll either go big or go home empty-handed. This is not a time to focus on developing relationships, as your major focus will be on your work.

You will feel pulled towards greed and corruption, having the sense that you must safeguard your achievements by accumulating more and more and locking it all up tightly. But the challenge of the 8 asks you to be ethical with your money. To embody the best of the 8, you'll need to find altruism and devote yourself to philanthropy. Otherwise, material gains may rot your spiritual side. Exercise balance and moderation during these years.

BALANCE NUMBER

We all react to challenges differently, both in our internal world and through our external actions. Some of us use a challenge as an opportunity to take stock of our approaches and reevaluate. Others may explode with emotion before reigning themselves in and getting back to it, while still others will let those feelings fester under the surface rather than show them at all.

Often, these responses are knee-jerk reactions that we don't analyze enough, but with maturity and a commitment to self-betterment, we can learn new, more effective ways of dealing with difficult situations. The balance number in numerology can provide guidance on how to do just that.

Our balance number is with us our whole life, but it remains dormant until it's needed. You'll feel the effects of this number most strongly when you're in emotional turmoil. The good news is that your balance number gives you everything you need to get your life... well, back into balance!

Calculating Your Balance Number

To calculate your balance number, use only your initials. Numerologists recommend using the initials in your full birth name. (For more about chosen names, refer back to the section on the numerology of name changes in Chapter Three).

Remove everything except the first letter of each word in your name. Then, using the Pythagorean alphanumeric cipher from Chapter One (and also at the beginning of the book under Resources), find the corresponding number for each letter and sum the resulting numbers.

Here's an example:

William Henry Abbot = W H A
W H A = 5 + 8 + 1 = 14 = 1 + 4 = 5

If your name ends in a "Jr.," "Sr.," or a Roman numeral like "III," ignore this in your calculations:

Martin Luther King, Jr. = M L K
M L K = 4 + 3 + 2 = 9

And reduce any master numbers, since they only apply to your core numbers and major cycles:

Ashley Anne Marie Wellington = A A M W
A A M W = 1 + 1 + 4 + 5 = 11 = 1 + 1 = 2

Calculate your own balance number and record the result in your chart. Now let's find the secrets to overcoming your life path's challenges.

The Way Through Adversity: What Your Balance Number Means for You

Balance 1

You must draw strength from within while *also* being more open to input from those you love. Don't face your problems alone – this will only lead to self-isolation when you need people the most. Talking through difficulties with others will help you gain a broader and more realistic perspective of your challenges.

Balance 2

Try to be less emotional and reactionary in the face of your challenges, instead relying on tact and diplomacy. You may find that you lack courage and are prone to avoiding confrontation, but if you trust in your own voice, you will find you have a knack for diffusing tensions. You must be willing to compromise and find the silver linings.

Balance 3

You must try to be more lighthearted in your approach to problems. Use your creative mind to dream up unexpected solutions, and try to let the little things roll off your back. Working alongside others to overcome an obstacle can lead to a mutually beneficial result, and you have all the charm necessary to make this a productive working relationship.

Balance 4

Self-discipline is your biggest strength. You must use it to control your anger in the face of setbacks. Be practical, not emotional. You are so in the nitty-gritty of life that you may forget to step back and look at the bigger picture. If you strive towards your ideals of justice and fairness, you may find compassion for someone you once saw as only an adversary.

Balance 5

You may find yourself prone to avoidance of conflict or turning away from your goals at the slightest setback. You must learn to face your problems head-on and avoid escapism, especially when it comes to indulging in food or drugs. You've cultivated a great perspective on life through all the new and different people you've met along the way. Use these lessons to find a creative solution to your challenges.

Balance 6

Your strength is in your ability to nurture relationships, but you cannot always rely on friends and family to provide solace when you're going through a difficult time. You must take the responsibility of fixing your problems into your own hands. Own your decisions, feel confident in your abilities to overcome adversity, and resist the temptation to retreat backwards into safety and comfort.

Balance 7

You have a rich inner world, which can act as a safe haven during difficult times. You must be careful not to lose yourself in this retreat. Your mind is sharp; you have everything you need to take the problem apart and put together a smart solution. You must confront yourself and explore the ways in which you create your own obstacles.

Balance 8

You're a powerful person, and when times are tough, you may be prone to using this power to manipulate others rather than deal with your disagreements directly. You're a problem solver, but you must focus on your *own* problems and avoid forcing your solutions onto others. If you maintain a balance between giving and receiving, you're well equipped to overcome whatever life throws at you.

Balance 9

Your empathy is your superpower, and developing this emotional skill will serve you well when it comes time to face your challenges. If you cultivate an understanding of others, you'll have a broad perspective and be able to see the problems you face at a higher level – and it's much easier to see the solution from this perspective! Be careful not to retreat from others when you're facing difficulties in life.

7

LOVE BY THE NUMBERS – NUMEROLOGY FOR RELATIONSHIPS

Numerology isn't *all* about self-reflection. You've seen the power inherent in single-digit numbers; now, let's learn how you can apply numerology to improve your romantic life.

COMPATIBILITY IN NUMEROLOGY

The principal way numerology can help with your relationships is by comparing the numbers in your chart with those in your partner's chart to see how compatible you are. Remember, numbers each have a distinct "personality," and these personalities can either clash or work harmoniously together.

There are many ways to look at compatibility, but we'll focus on two reference points in your chart: your life path and soul urge numbers.

Life Path Compatibility

As you now know, your life path is one of the most essential numbers in your chart, so it follows that it's an essential number to consider when calculating your compatibility with a partner. If you two are on completely opposite paths in life, you're probably not going to ride off into the sunset together. The truth is that while you may be able to teach each other some valuable lessons, you have two very different places to be!

The chart below displays the highest and lowest compatibility ratings among life paths. Find your life path and your partner's. For the sake of compatibility, reduce any master numbers to their single-digit form.

	1	2	3	4	5	6	7	8	9
1	Low		High		High	High		Low	Low
2			Low	High	Low	High		High	
3	High	Low	Low	Low	High	Low		Low	High
4		High	Low		Low		High	High	Low
5	High	Low	High	Low			High	Low	Low
6	High	High	Low				Low	High	High
7				High	High	Low	High	Low	Low
8	Low	High	Low	High	Low	High	Low		Low
9	Low		High	Low	Low	High	Low	Low	High

Soul Urge Compatibility

As you've learned here, your soul urge number highlights your innermost heart's desires. This is crucial in a serious relationship. Your personalities may perfectly complement one another, but if your core values – what you *really want* out of life – aren't aligned, you're bound for a rocky relationship road.

The chart below displays the highest and lowest compatibility ratings among soul urge numbers. Find your soul urge and your partner's. Again, reduce any master numbers to their single-digit form.

	1	2	3	4	5	6	7	8	9
1			High		High		High	Low	High
2			High	High		High		High	
3	High	High	High	Low	High	High		Low	High
4		High	Low		Low	High	High	High	Low
5		Low	High	Low	High	Low	High	Low	High
6	Low	High	High	High	Low			Low	High
7	High		High	High	High			Low	
8	Low	High		High		Low			Low
9	High		High	Low	High	High		Low	

RELATIONSHIP NUMBER

Compatibility comparison, in numerology as well as in astrology and some other disciplines, can be a little abstract and generic. But the relationship number speaks *directly* to the relationship in question.

This number doesn't appear in your numerological chart, but it reveals a *lot* – not just about you, but about your relationship with your partner (or friend, or potential partner), because it's calculated using numbers from *both* of your charts.

Calculating Your Relationship Number

You'll need your partner's full name and date of birth to do this – or, alternatively, their life path and expression numbers. Finding this number involves making several calculations, so concentrate and get out your notebook!

First, add your life path and expression number and reduce it to a single digit. Do the same for your partner's life path and expression numbers. Sum these two numbers together and reduce them again (if needed) to find your relationship number. Reduce any master numbers you encounter.

If you need to refresh your memory on how to calculate the life path and expression numbers, return to Chapters Two and Three for guidance.

For example, if your life path is 1 and your expression is 3 and your partner's life path is 2 and their expression 7, your relationship number is 4, like so:

$$1 + 3 = 4$$
$$2 + 7 = 9$$
$$4 + 9 = 13 = 1 + 3 = 4$$

What Your Relationship Number Reveals About You and Your Partner

Relationship 1

You are a "power couple!" This relationship will thrive if you have something big to focus on together. You both have incredible skills that, when combined, will take you to new heights.

If you are struggling in your relationship, take stock of where the focus is and shift it back to your shared dreams. Make plans for the future and try something new together to ignite the fire.

Relationship 2

Communication is key to the success of this relationship. Whether or not you are individually skilled in communication, you must endeavor to speak your heart to your partner and listen to them in return.

If you are struggling in your relationship, things may be out of balance. Are you giving more than you're taking? Is there a compromise to be made?

Relationship 3

Your relationship is a playful, joyous one. You let your inner child out around each other and seek adventure together. Your relationship is at its strongest when you're living life to the fullest with your partner by your side.

If you are struggling in your relationship, look to bring *fun* back into it. Let go of routine and try something spontaneous.

Relationship 4

Your relationship grounds you. You work well together, as long as you keep your home life organized and routines in place, even if you are not an organized person yourself. Your relationship depends on this.

If you are struggling in your relationship, take a look at its practical foundation. Is there something in your home life that's unbalanced, like a uneven division of chores or finances?

Relationship 5

A relationship of 5 will thrive when you have adventures with your partner! You need to keep things fresh and exciting, so play up spontaneity, and don't forget to give each other some healthy space.

If you are struggling in your relationship, try something new. Take a trip together... or just rearrange the bedroom.

Relationship 6

In this relationship, you and your partner are each other's sanctuary. You create a loving space together in which anything is possible.

If your relationship is facing struggles, ensure you are appropriately nurturing it. You do a good job of taking care of each other, but what about taking care of yourselves *together*? Take stock of the things you do for your partner and ensure you're not out of balance.

Relationship 7

This relationship promises a deep soul connection. It's likely that you're in your own world of two and that you know each other inside and out.

If you are struggling in your relationship, make sure you're being vulnerable and authentic with your partner and that they're doing the same. If you fall into routine small-talk, the passion will wane.

Relationship 8

This relationship is all about the balance of power, both financial and personal. Together, the two of you have incredible potential, but you'll need regular check-ins and honesty to ensure one of you doesn't get ahead of the other.

If your relationship is struggling, take a look at the power dynamic. Is one person in charge of everything? Does one bring in all the money? Shake things up and see how you feel.

Relationship 9

Your relationship was destined to happen! With the 9 representing the end of the cycle, you've been brought together to end a pattern you've been playing out in life. You and your partner work harmoniously together to make the world a better place.

If you are struggling in your relationship, take some time off for yourselves. Go on a trip together and explore that intimate one-on-one connection.

LUCKY NUMBERS – NUMEROLOGY FOR SUCCESS

How fortuitous that our chapter on harnessing numerology for personal success is the eighth chapter in the book!

As we've learned, the 8 is the most prosperous number in numerology. Some numerologists have even been known to change their names specifically to get more 8s in their chart. But 8 isn't the *only* number that signals good fortune.

If you're curious to know how you can harness the power of numbers to drive your own success, don't worry – you don't need to change your name. Instead, you can use the power of numbers to help you do things like find auspicious dates to make money moves, come up with a prosperous name for your new start-up company, or choose the most rewarding route when multiple options are presented to you.

LUCKY NUMBERS

There is no one-size-fits-all approach to numerology for success; it is personal to you. Numerologists derive your lucky numbers from your life path, but there isn't really any calculation involved. Instead, we'll examine the *series* of numbers that corresponds to your life path number.

Though we reduce double-digit numbers when they show up in our numerological charts, in the real world, multiple-digit numbers appear everywhere. A series in numerology refers to all the numbers that spring from a single digit. For example, consider how both 51 and 33 reduce to 6 using our numerological calculations. Thus, if your life path number is 6, all the numbers in series 6 are considered lucky for you.

If your life path number is one of the master numbers, reduce it; you'll see it listed under the corresponding series.

Series 1: 1, 10, 19, 28, 37, 46, 55, 64, 73, 82, 91
Series 2: 2, 11, 20, 29, 38, 47, 56, 65, 74, 83, 92
Series 3: 3, 12, 21, 30, 39, 48, 57, 66, 75, 84, 93

Series 4: 4, 13, 22, 31, 40, 49, 58, 67, 76, 85, 94
Series 5: 5, 14, 23, 32, 41, 50, 59, 68, 77, 86, 95
Series 6: 6, 15, 24, 33, 42, 51, 60, 69, 78, 87, 96
Series 7: 7, 16, 25, 34, 43, 52, 61, 70, 79, 88, 97
Series 8: 8, 17, 26, 35, 44, 53, 62, 71, 80, 89, 98
Series 9: 9, 18, 27, 36, 45, 54, 63, 72, 81, 90, 99

Numbers in series 8, as you may have guessed, are considered especially fortunate for material success. This is why those born under a life path of 8 are so blessed (and yet also challenged). But each series brings its own unique tidings related to the energy of the corresponding single-digit number. The 2 series, for example, is especially fortunate when it comes to relationships and the 7 series, for spiritual seeking.

We'll take a closer look at some of the series that are best for business and career success: 5, 6, 8, and 9.

Series 5

The number 5 is sometimes called the "universal benefactor" because regardless of your life path, numbers in this series are lucky for everyone in every endeavor, except marriage. Recall the energy of the 5: wild and free. A great number for taking financial risks, but not especially positive for a romantic entanglement!

The 23 is a particularly lucky number in this series, and is considered by some to be the most powerful number in numerology. Similarly, 32 holds great promise, as it correlates with wide appeal to the public. Both of these make an excellent number for business endeavors, and many Fortune 500 companies have names that sum to a number in series 5.

Series 6

You may recall that the 6 is all about service to others and that at its best, all the wonderful things the 6 gives out return to it tenfold. So, too, series 6 promises significant rewards for those who practice care in business.

The 33 is an especially fortunate number, the master teacher and the "number of the Lord of Wealth." Those born under a 6 life path will reap the most from the 33, but anyone can benefit from this supremely lucky number.

The 51 is also uniquely poised to bring good fortune. It represents the strength of the human soul and corresponds with many of the top businesses in the Fortune 500.

Series 8

The 8 series is a little trickier than 5 and 6. Those who were not born with a life path of 8 would do well to steer clear of the numbers in this series. While they can bring great success, there is also a higher risk of failure. If you stake your fortune on one of these numbers, be sure you've carefully considered such a move.

Of the 8 series, 44 and 53 are particularly good for wealth. Exxon Mobile and Microsoft give these numbers, respectively, from the sum of the letters in their business names.

Series 9

You may recall that the 9 represents the completion of a cycle and all the wisdom that comes along with a full journey through numbers 1-9. It makes sense, then, that the 9 series is particularly fortuitous. Anyone can harness the power of this series, although those with a life path of 9 are best poised for success from these numbers.

The 27 and 45 represent divinity, 27 being a sacred number in occult circles. These numbers will bring good fortune, not only in business but in all aspects of life.

The 18, however, is often considered bad for relationships and should not be used as a lucky number in most circumstances.

FINAL WORDS

If you've followed along throughout the book, congratulations: you've created your own numerological chart! You understand the meanings inherent in each number and why they are endowed with their particular energy. You know how each number in your chart applies to who you are as a person (the good *and* the not so good), what your path in life is all about, the challenges you'll face, and the ways you'll grow and change. You've also learned how numbers can influence your relationships and help you achieve financial success.

You have at your fingertips everything you need to succeed in life. Continue self-reflection, keep striving to be the best version of yourself, and your new knowledge of numerology will always be there to help you harness your own incredible strengths.

I believe in you – and so do the numbers!

9 781957 710082